THE INCENDIARY FELLOWSHIP

Other books by Elton Trueblood

THE PEOPLE CALLED QUAKERS
THE LORD'S PRAYERS
THE HUMOR OF CHRIST
GENERAL PHILOSOPHY
THE COMPANY OF THE COMMITTED
CONFRONTING CHRIST
THE YOKE OF CHRIST
PHILOSOPHY OF RELIGION
THE RECOVERY OF FAMILY LIFE
YOUR OTHER VOCATION
THE LIFE WE PRIZE
THE COMMON VENTURES OF LIFE
ALTERNATIVE TO FUTILITY
FOUNDATIONS FOR RECONSTRUCTION
THE PREDICAMENT OF MODERN MAN

The Incendiary Fellowship

Elton Trueblood
PROFESSOR AT LARGE
EARLHAM COLLEGE

Published in San Francisco by

HARPER & ROW, PUBLISHERS

New York, Hagerstown, San Francisco, London

First Harper & Row paperback edition published in 1978.

The text of this book is printed on 100% recycled paper.

Library of Congress Cataloging in Publication Data

Trueblood, David Elton, 1900—
   The incendiary fellowship

   Bibliographical footnotes.

   1. Church.   2. Christianity—20th cent.   I. Title.

BV 640.T7   260   67-11508

ISBN 0-06-068641-3 pbk.

78 79 80 81 82 10 9 8 7 6 5 4 3 2 1

To Elizabeth
with a
father's affection

Contents

PREFACE

The more I think about it, the more I am convinced that Christ was proposing a fellowship more radical in its essential nature than it has been conventional to suppose. Far from glorifying the temple and its ritual, he said explicitly that "Something greater than the temple is here" (Matt. 12:6). He left the synagogue and soon afterward sent out a team of workers, not to perform a ceremony, but to liberate and to heal (Mark 6:7-13). Instead of employing priests, He entrusted the future to ordinary persons; He built His Church, not upon an elite class, but upon men as weak as Simon Peter (Matt. 16:18), predicting that this strange foundation would be able to resist the powers of death. Subsequent history has confirmed His prediction.

Nearly all of Christ's metaphors concerning the Church are ones of penetration. Christians are called, not to separation from the world, but to the kind of activity which enables salt to preserve meat from decay. The Church is intended, not as something concerned with its own preservation, but as a light which, in penetrating the darkness, is *expended*. The life of the Church is saved only by being lost! The yeast of the Church exists, not to be maintained, but to be consumed in the dough as it rises and becomes more edible.

It is evident that Christ's awareness of the enigmatic nature of His radical redemptive proposal motivated His sustained attempt to clarify it. How else can we understand Christ's repeated use of phrases such as "I came" or "I have come," which are clearly intended to explain His fundamental purpose? This is how Luke 12:49, "I come to cast fire upon the earth," achieves the fullness of its meaning. It is best understood when seen as only one of the "I cames," though the most vivid of them all. It is the one statement of purpose which modern Christians most need to understand if they are to envision the true character of their calling as Christ's representatives in the world.

Like the first followers, we easily miss the novelty of Christ's proposal of the means by which the world may be penetrated and saved. If we are not careful we tend to fall back into pre-Christian expectations of religious activity, thereby missing the exciting nature of the redemptive society in which we are called to participate. We share the holy task of reminding ourselves and one another of how hot the fire is intended to be. Part of that task is to help one another to remember that Christ came, not to propose mild religious innovation, but to cast fire upon the earth. Inadequate kindling as we are, we are nevertheless called to be the components of the conflagration.

We have rightly emphasized, during the past quarter century, the theme of Church Renewal—perhaps the most hopeful topic of our century. This theme can never be exhausted, because the need for it remains. We dare not be satisfied with mere maintenance of an operation, advance and decay being the only options open to mankind. But we cannot be effective in renewal if we are not clear about the nature of the dream which possesses us.

The hymn "Baptism by Fire" is my best effort to present, in poetic form, the vision of what the true character of Christ's Church would be if we could accept the magnitude of His original design. The hymn is now being widely used, having already appeared in several hymnals, including the *Covenant Hymnal* and that of the United Presbyterian Church. Though several different musical settings have been suggested, the words are most often matched to the Welsh tune *Hyfrydol*. My hope is that the poetry will prepare readers for the prose which follows, and help to make people dissatisfiied with anything less than a New Pentecost.

E. T.

Earlham
June, 1978

Baptism By Fire

(Hymn)

I

Thou, whose purpose is to kindle:
Now ignite us with Thy fire;
While the earth awaits Thy burning
With Thy passion us inspire.
Overcome our sinful calmness,
Rouse us with redemptive shame;
Baptize with Thy fiery Spirit,
Crown our lives with tongues of flame.

II

Thou, who, in Thy holy Gospel,
Wills that man should truly live:
Make us sense our share of failure,
Our tranquility forgive.
Teach us courage as we struggle
In all liberating strife;
Lift the smallness of our vision,
By Thine own abundant life.

III

Thou, who still a sword delivers,
Rather than a placid peace:
With Thy sharpened word disturb us,
From complacency, release!
Save us now from satisfaction,
When we privately are free,
Yet are undisturbed in spirit,
By our brother's misery.

THE INCENDIARY FELLOWSHIP

CHAPTER 1

A Contemporary Christian Delusion

If we could first know where we are, and whither we are tending, we could better judge what to do and how to do it.
—Abraham Lincoln

Committed Christians are a minority at the present time! This is true, not merely in the world at large, but in the Western world as well, and specifically in the United States of America. Though there is a widespread failure to understand this significant fact, the evidence for it is abundant. A great part of the weakness of the Christian movement stems from the miscalculation both of its strength and of the degree of its acceptance. Consequently, the wisdom of Lincoln's famous aphorism is the wisdom which we need at this juncture. Realism is the only feasible starting point for advance.

As we study the New Testament we soon realize that part of the power of the early Christian Movement arose from the clear recognition that it was by no means popular or generally accepted. The hope of reaching the masses with a redemptive power was always prefaced by the clear recognition that the opposition was intense as well as abundant. Thus the Apostle Paul reported that "a wide door for effective work has opened to me, and there are many adversaries" (I Cor. 16:9).[1] When Paul and his teammates first entered the cities of the Greek mainland they

[1] Unless otherwise stated, all Biblical references are to the Revised Standard Version.

were totally surrounded by both the uncomprehending and the contemptuous. Naturally the people asked, "What would this babbler say?" (Acts 17:18).

The contempt and ridicule which the early Christians encountered had been predicted accurately by their Lord, who had urged them to rejoice when persecuted. "Blessed are you when men hate you, and when they exclude you and revile you, and cast out your name as evil, on account of the Son of man!" (Luke 6:22). Since opposition was expected, the early Christians prepared themselves for it. Whatever their mistakes, they were at least not guilty of a weakening optimism, because they understood perfectly that the only reasonable way to face a minority status is the way of inner toughness. Thus we have the striking admonition, "You must therefore be like men stripped for action" (I Pet. 1:13, NEB). It is only when we see this necessary consequence that we truly appreciate the military metaphors which mark the New Testament.

In many ways contemporary Christians are less fortunate than were the Christians of the first century. And the paradox is that part of our misfortune stems from some degree of Christian success. Working against incredible odds, the Gospel impressed itself upon the ancient Greco-Roman culture, and vestiges of this impression remain to this day. Christian ideas have penetrated the law, the governments, the educational systems, the secular literature. The Church of Christ, though fragmented, still appears to be powerful, sometimes having a direct influence on governments and sometimes taking leadership in social action. People who are not Christians, in any sense of the word, expect to find Christian references in literature and they generally understand them.[2] It would be a highly illiterate person who would be entirely mystified by a reference to Golgotha. The very familiarity with the Christian terms makes it harder for people to take them seriously. They are old hat.

---

[2] Thus there is no problem in catching the Gospel reference in the speech of Hamlet (Act V, sc. 2) from which the epigraph of Chap. 3 is taken. The reference to the fall of the sparrow is specifically Christian.

Perhaps it is the physical evidence of the Church which most lends credence to the delusion that Christians enjoy a majority status. The alien visitor quickly notices the abundance of ecclesiastical buildings. The average city sky-line is still marked by the presence of spires and, in spite of rising land prices, prominent sites are still occupied by church buildings. The fact that these are not taxed seems to be a mark of general public acceptance. Moreover, the wealth represented by other kinds of church property is great and is becoming greater. Though there has been erosion in the Christian colleges, a great many of our older colleges are still owned by supporting denominations.

The revelation of our true status, so far as buildings are concerned, may be facilitated by a consideration of the mosques of Istanbul. These mosques provide the tourist with his most impressive sight, partly because they are so numerous and partly because they are so obvious, but even the casual visitor soon learns what a small role these stunning buildings play in the contemporary life of the great city by the Bosphorus. Physical appearances may be highly deceptive, especially in something as important as religion. External evidences may go on for a long time after the power of a religion to influence the masses has largely ended.

The fact that committed Christians are only a minority is hidden from us, in part, by the supposedly widespread practice of attending public worship, particularly on Sundays. It is often those who do not attend who believe, most uncritically, that the practice of attendance is nearly universal, when actually it is far from being so. In some parts of continental Europe and England there are areas in which there is practically no attendance at all. I have, personally, counted eight people in a magnificent building at eleven o'clock on Sunday morning. The habit of nonattendance has already hit the eastern seaboard of the United States and is now moving both west and south.

It must be clearly understood that the minority status which we are beginning to recognize refers specifically to a committed Christianity and not to a vague religiosity. Of this latter there is undoubtedly a great deal. It is marked by the continuance of official "membership" and by the use of the facilities of the Church in connection with baptism, marriage, and death. These observances go on for a long time, even when the central fire has been almost extinguished, for there is a world of difference between a committed Christianity and the presence of marrying and burying parsons in a community. If the latter were sufficient, it would be reasonable to say of the Western world what the Apostle Paul said to the Athenians, "I perceive that in every way you are very religious" (Acts 17:22).

We cannot be rightly prepared for the fierce struggle of our generation if we do not understand the intensity of the opposition to a committed Christianity. Part of the opposition stems from the built-in naturalism which, with many, is a matter of unconscious or unstated assumptions. The very success of natural science had led millions to suppose that causal determinism is a philosophy which applies to every aspect of the real world. Miracle is therefore ruled out *a priori*. The miracle of the resurrection of Christ is rejected, not because the evidence for it is inadequate or faulty, but because of a dogmatic position which is incompatible with such an event. The idea that the divine purposive order is superior to the order of natural law is an idea which, for millions, is not consciously rejected, simply because it has never been entertained.

. The popular determinism is applied even to acts of human decision. Though a few see that this involves logical difficulties, in that it utterly destroys any rational basis of responsibility, it appears that the majority accept their naturalism uncritically. This leads to the sentimentality in which all acts are "explained" and renders meaningless the conception of sin. We have not faced adequately the degree to which such a position stands in direct contrast to the entire Christian understanding of the human situation. A different philosophy may be a real barrier, and it is especially so when it is based upon premises which are unargued, because they are unexamined.

In earlier days it seemed reasonable to speak of "Comparative

Religions," meaning Buddhism, Christianity, Islam, Judaism, etc. No longer, however, are these, for most people, the live options. A truly contemporary course in comparative religions would deal with naturalism, dialectical materialism, and the new paganism. The new paganism, which differs in important ways from the classic paganism of Greece and Rome, is now becoming an explicit and self-conscious faith. This faith has important evangelistic organs, such as *Playboy* and *Esquire,* and the doctrines are receiving progressively sharper expression as the leaders enunciate them.

A good introduction to the new faith may be the reading of a recent issue of *Esquire* in which several articles set out the creed which is presented as a clear alternative to Christianity. One author, who has experienced four marriages, explains that the Christian vow of lifelong fidelity to one mate is a wholly outmoded idea. There is, he says, nothing sacred about it, and, indeed, there is nothing sacred about anything. The only "ought," apparently, is that one ought not to be inhibited in any way. The moral philosophy is that of complete and unlimited self-expression or self-satisfaction. How many there are who subscribe to this oversimplified creed we have no way of knowing, but there is every reason to believe that the number is very large.

When we call this particular paganism something new we must be careful not to be understood as saying that sin is new. Of course it is not! What is new is that so many people now make a conscious glorification of what others have seen as shameful. For thousands today infidelity is not something for which anyone has any reason to be ashamed; instead it is to be encouraged. What is novel is not the act, but the ideology. And the preaching of a doctrine is always a greater potential danger than is an act, since the doctrine is an enterprise in multiplication. The doctrine is significant because it persuades others to follow suit. While paganism is something which we have always had in one form or another, it has now become evangelical. It was given explicit expression by the late Ernest Hemingway in the famous novelist's doctrine of "feelings."[3] However confused this doctrine may be, it is important to realize that it is not really strange in the modern world, since all that it does is to carry the principle of subjectivity to its logical limit. Finally the break with God, and with an objective moral law, is complete. But the thoughtful person must face the consequences. One consequence is that, if the kidnaper feels good after the kidnaping, the act is moral. Only the truly unsophisticated will doubt that this is a possibility. Because the human being is adept at the creation of the easy conscience, he can make himself feel good about almost anything. The pagan, because he is fundamentally naïve, does not know this, but the interpreters of the Gospel of Christ have always known it, because the Gospel is realistic about the human situation.

If we watch for the evidences we can see the marks of the new paganism without taking the trouble to visit a booth at Berkeley, California, for it appears even in news reports. For example, in the Associated Press report of the fourth marriage of a popular motion picture actor, the actor is quoted as providing an explanation of why the marriage was at first kept secret. "We kept it secret," he is reported as saying, "because marriage is a very private affair." This is the exact antithesis of the Christian idea of marriage, the Church having always insisted upon the public character of the sacred undertaking. Marriage is intrinsically public, Christians assert, because we are part of a fellowship, and also because there are many consequent public responsibilities. This is poles apart from the adolescent idea that marriage exists only for the private self-indulgence of the two partners.

One of the new alternatives to Christianity is the cult of L.S.D. That this is a cult is beyond argument, for there is a ritualistic

[3] As usually repeated, in the books of quotations, the formula is: "So far, about morals, I know only that what is moral is what you feel good after and what is immoral is what you feel bad after." However, in fairness, it ought to be said that Hemingway added, "judged by these moral standards, which I do not defend. . . ." *Death in the Afternoon* (New York: Charles Scribner's Sons, 1932), p. 4. Even the reader who desires to be fair, and thus includes the denial, will note the inner contradiction.

way in which the drug is taken. Some of the adherents of the new cult have stressed its religious character by claiming that any limitation on their use of the drug would involve a denial of the freedom of religion guaranteed by the First Amendment to the Constitution of the United States. But when we recognize the cult as "religious" we must be critical enough to realize that it includes not even a hint of the compassion and social consciousness which have been intrinsic to Christianity from the beginning. The drugtaker may see visions, but his religion is not likely to involve the dynamism of those who were led to oppose slavery because the slave, like the freeman, is a child of the Living God and one for whom Christ died.

Though the new evangelical paganism makes much of sincerity, it is easy to see that it is marked, to an unusual degree, by cant and pretense. At the same time that its exponents reject any moral order, claiming to be released from "Puritanism," they denounce university officials as "unfair" when they do not provide birth control pills for unmarried girls. It is obviously self-contradictory to deny, on the one hand, the existence of an objective moral order and yet, on the other, to engage in moral denunciation of any body or anything, yet the new pagans make denunciation and harsh judgment their stock in trade. Their emancipation thus includes liberation from the necessity of logical consistency.

Even in the new paganism there are strange vestiges of a Christian world view. Though the high priests of the movement claim vociferously that they belong to a post-Christian age, they still do not adopt the complete ruthlessness which would be the logical consequence of their position. Sexual intercourse, a subject to which they return again and again, is said to be all right between any man and woman, married or unmarried, *so long as no one is hurt*. This looks, on the surface, amazingly similar to the Christian concern which is held in such contempt. And this is undoubtedly the source of the limitation, for it is through the Christian Gospel that the idea of respect for the individual came into the world. But we may wonder at the naïveté of those who

ch a standard so lightly. Can we be so sure, when illicit
e occurs, who is hurt and how deep the hurt is? There
are other forms of hurt besides unwanted pregnancy. Only a
superman could know for sure whether there is any hurt.

When we recognize how numerous the alternatives are, we are
not really surprised that Christianity is a minority movement,
even in the heart of the West. In addition to the systems already
mentioned there is the cult of the New Left, and racism, and the
various forms of militant nationalism. But the greatest single
alternative is that of a conventionalized association with the
Christian heritage which is best described as mild religion. There
is no doubt that this accounts for the largest part of the nominal
memberships in the local churches. This mild Christianity is
largely separated from the Bible, which seems to many to be
more of a burden than a help.

Nearly all of the representatives of mild Christianity think of
themselves as anti-Puritan, though the number of these who
really know what the dynamic Puritan faith was in the seventeenth century seems to be few. To caricature the Puritan ethic
and to reject it without genuine examination is particularly
inept, especially when we think of the central fire represented by
John Milton, whose creative freedom arose, not in spite of, but as
a consequence of his disciplined faith.

The standard rejection of the Puritan ideal is only one facet of
a general view of life which makes a fetish out of personal liberty. The person whose overreaching desire is for his own personal liberty will naturally be anti-Church, because he cannot
fail to see that genuine church membership involves heavy
responsibilities, which limit one's personal whims. In a very per-
ceptive interview Dean Robert E. Fitch, of the Pacific School of
Religion, reports that he frequently runs into groups of people
who say, "Well, we don't like churches. We don't like worship.
After all, religion is a very private and personal matter. It's
nobody else's business. It's just between me and God." Dean
Fitch makes the following rejoinder: "Well, of course religion
ought to be personal, but if it's nothing but personal, it's some-

thing brand new in history. There never was any purely personal religion, in the whole history of the world, except for a few isolated mystics."[4]

The love of liberty is a very great thing and it has always been part of the Christian faith, but the liberty of the Christian man has been vastly more than a concern for his own freedom in isolation from the structures of society and the Church. It is the Christian concern for freedom that has produced such remarkable results as the emancipation of women and the legal cessation of human slavery. But the Christian philosophy of freedom has always involved discipline as its price. The original statement of this philosophy appears in the words of Christ which are frequently quoted in part, but seldom quoted in their totality, "If you continue in my word, you are truly my disciples, and you will know the truth, and the truth will make you free (John 8:31, 32). In other words, according to Christ, freedom is not a starting point, but always a conclusion; it is something to be earned. And the participation in the life of the disciplined and committed group is part of the price. This is what those who are satisfied with mild religion do not know. They do not wholly reject the Church, and are even glad that it exists, but they look upon it as an institution in the community which offers certain services of which they may avail themselves from time to time. The Church, in short, is *useful*. But they are terribly shy of anything that looks like urgency or fanatical devotion. This is one reason why the New Testament seems to them to be a strange and often repellent book.

We are coming close now to an understanding of the paradox of the majority and minority status of Christianity in the West. It is the prevalence of mild religion which gives credibility to the notion that Christianity is the dominant faith. But it is delusion, nevertheless, because this is only a caricature of the religion of Jesus Christ. It is those who are passionately devoted to Christ and His Kingdom who constitute a minority. But it is a minority

[4] "Is America Ready for a 'Great Society'?" *U.S. News and World Report* (March 8, 1965), p. 54.

which is always powerful and can become more powerful through a clear understanding of its true situation. The reasonable hope is that many who come to see the contrast between the mild religion which has hitherto satisfied them and a truly committed Christianity, will be impelled to change.

Though there is no need at this point to essay a full description of a committed Christianity, it may be said briefly that what is meant is a faith marked by a burning conviction and the consequent desire to see it spread. It is the exact opposite of mild religion with its easy tolerance. Committed Christianity is radically different from "religion in general," being based on a conviction which is definite. In the most profound sense of the word it is "narrow" and it is unapologetically so. A Christian is committed to the conviction that God really is, that He is wholly personal, that He is like Jesus Christ, and that God has a particular interest in each individual of the human race. We do not deny that there are good people who reject every item of the faith just mentioned. What we affirm is that this is what Christianity is. The person who claims to be a Christian while rejecting such convictions is simply engaging in a contradiction of terms. That the Christian Way is intrinsically narrow is the clear affirmation of part of the Sermon on the Mount: "For the gate is narrow and the way is hard, that leads to life, and those who find it are few" (Matt. 7:14).

If we could have a renewed understanding of these unequivocal words of Christ, we should have a brave start on Church Renewal. The lines are beginning to be drawn and this may be a good thing, for there is a world of difference between the frank acceptance of a narrow way, and the popular notion that one way is as good as another. The pressure to conform to the broad way is now very strong and is getting stronger. For example, there are cities in which the Y.M.C.A. is urged to drop the word "Christian" from its name, and at least one financial drive has failed because of refusal to do so. It is important to note that the chief pressure has not come from Jews, but from those whose only religious expression is a vague goodwill. The resistance is not specifically to Christianity, but to anything which has a sharpness of outline. Before Christians succumb to such pressures they are wise to note that there is no cutting edge that is not narrow. There is no likelihood whatever that Christianity could have won in the ancient world as religion in general. It survived very largely because it accepted the scandal of particularity. It could not have survived had it not been sufficiently definite to be counted worthy of persecution.

A tolerant pantheism, which is the real core of some of the self-styled new theology, will never be persecuted because most people will never oppose anything so vague. What people oppose is the conviction that God really is, that Christ was telling the truth when He said, "No one comes to the Father, but by me" (John 14:6), and that God's purpose involves moral distinctions. People naturally resist the conception of an objective moral order, finding it far more comfortable to suppose that all moral laws have only subjective reference and can therefore be neglected with impunity. We are missing the point terribly if we do not see that a faith which is as definite as the Gospel of Christ is now and always will be a stone of stumbling and an occasion of offense. Because the sharp line is never popular, we are foolish to expect it to be so. Those who try to follow the narrow way must expect to be part of a minority all of their lives.

The committed Christian is not now thrown to the lions, as were the Christians in Rome long ago, but there are nevertheless, subtle forms of contemporary persecution. A man who takes Christ seriously is often looked upon as a hopeless fossil and is considered an enthusiast or a fanatic. In short, he is an oddity. This is not because Christian values are entirely rejected in the contemporary world. Indeed, there are many evidences which show that several Christian values survive for a while after the abandonment of the faith from which they first emerged. A striking illustration of this is seen in the contemporary drive for social justice. Much of this effort clearly stems from Christian roots even though the connection with those roots has now been severed.

It would be foolish to deny that many of the characteristic men and women of our age are decent people. Though they would find it fairly laughable if they were accused of being unapologetic agents of Jesus Christ in the world, they are often fair, and they try to be just. Though we do have, in our time of unparalleled affluence, a striking rise in the crime rate, most of the people are not criminals. They give to the community chest; they maintain an uncostly membership in some church; they have some degree of fidelity to their marriage vows. Very few of these people would steal your purse if you made the mistake of leaving it behind and not many are extreme in cheating the government of its lawful revenue. The strange fact is that these people, who constitute the obvious majority, are almost universally opposed to the kind of Christianity represented by the New Testament. The claims are too strong; the price is too high; the fire of evangelism is too hot. The crucial fact is that all evangelism is faintly embarrassing. The spirit of the Book of Acts makes us uncomfortable. We are discomfited by the young Mormon missionaries who come to town and we find it necessary to minimize the effectiveness of Billy Graham. Though the New Testament describes a hot fire, we prefer the damp wick.

One possible response to the minority status of the Christians is for interpreters of the Gospel to try to make the Gospel conform to what the world already respects. Thus we are told very loudly that Christians must give up all of their ancient language, including the language used by Christ Himself. The advice is that we must no longer speak of sin, though we can perhaps speak of maladjustment. We must not speak of truth, for that is too harsh. There are high officials in the churches who now express the view that the Christian message must be altered to make it acceptable to the men and women who, they affirm, live in a wholly new age.

It is time to challenge the confident talk about the radical discontinuity between our generation and all preceding ones. It is true, of course, that we move physically with greater speed, but this is only one phase of the total situation. A little thought should make us aware that a man can hate his wife just as much while traveling six hundred miles an hour as when traveling six. We have, indeed, some education, but only the very immature suppose that we are consequently wise. Furthermore, technical knowledge does not necessarily make men good or compassionate or loyal. It is time for someone to say clearly that the ultimate human situation has not changed at all. Undoubtedly, we shall place men on the moon, but only the naïve could suppose that such a feat would alter human motives. All thoughtful readers can be grateful to James Burnham for making this essential point so forthrightly. "Educated people," says Burnham, "have inward drives, greeds, compulsions, passions and a lust for power that are not eliminated by any known process of education."[5]

The truth is that modern man is overimpressed by his own achievements. To put a rocket into an orbit that is more than a hundred miles from the surface of the earth takes a great deal of joint thought and effort, but we tend to overstate the case. Though the men who ride a few miles above the earth are called astronauts, this is clearly a misnomer. Men will not be astronauts until they ride among the stars, and it is important to remember that most of the stars are thousands of light-years away. The Russians are even more unrestrained in their overstatement, calling their men cosmonauts. Someone needs to say, "Little man, don't take yourself quite so seriously."

It is clear that if Christians are to bring the power of Jesus Christ to the world, they must make themselves understood, and this involves difficult intellectual labor, but this is not the same as making the lines fuzzy in order to render the Gospel acceptable. We are far more effective if we know that the Gospel will never be entirely acceptable, and that the Christian Movement will continue to be a minority movement. The Gospel must seek to penetrate the world and all of its parts, but it cannot do so unless there is a sense in which it is in contrast to the world. Herein lies the central paradox.

The denial of the paradox comes in many ways, the chief of which is the increasing tendency of the Church to be identical

---

[5] Quoted in *World Aflame* by Billy Graham (Garden City, N.Y.: Doubleday & Co., Inc., 1965), p. xiv.

with the world. To many outsiders the Church appears to be a thriving business, the appearance of worldly success being accentuated by our constant emphasis upon promotion. The pastor often becomes more a business executive than anything else, with the operation seeming to center on the mortgage or the budget. People who are urged to give to God are naturally disturbed when they find that they are chiefly giving to human salaries. Those who attend worship out of a deep sense of personal need are often disappointed when they note the importance of the announcements and realize the extent to which these are frankly promotional. Attendance is being whipped up for the next meeting or the next dinner.

The stranger who is visited by a representative of the Church frequently gets the impression that he is being viewed as a prospective customer, a potential addition to the numbers or the income, rather than a person who is approached for his own sake. Part of the shame of the contemporary Church is that it seems to be motivated by self-interest. We need to be reminded that the Church exists for men and not men for the Church.

One of the great theological gains of the twentieth century has been the widespread recognition of the necessity of the Church in any vital Christianity, a clear statement of the new theological consensus about the importance of the Church being that of Stephen Neill. "Theologically," he says, "we have been discovering anew that the Church is not an appendage to the Gospel; it is itself a part of the Gospel. The Gospel cannot be separated from that new people of God in which its nature is to be made manifest."[6] The fellowship is intrinsic and is never optional, if the life of Christ is to make an impact on the world. But it is possible for the Church to exist, with a show of success, and still fail in its essential function. It is always failing when it becomes an institution which is bent on saving itself. It cannot save the world if it demonstrates an obsession with material things.

When the pastor is an entrepreneur and the Church is a busi-

[6] *Christian Faith and Other Faiths* (London: Oxford University Press, 1961), p. 206.

ness, the Christian community develops a majority consciousness and thereby ceases to be the saving salt. As Christ predicted, it is easy for the salt to be dissolved away. Without its salty character the Church is not good for anything, because it has lost its reason for being. To be distinctive it must recognize its minority status and accept the consequences of that recognition. What the world desperately needs is a redemptive fellowship centered in Jesus Christ, as an antidote to the evils of civilization. The problem is not that of organizing a congregation, which is easy, but rather that of seeing to it that the salt does not lose its savor. The crucial question now, as in the beginning, is "How shall its saltness be restored?" (Luke 14:34).

We are fortunate, in our time, in that a number of thinkers are giving serious and urgent attention to the ancient question. We now have several books devoted to the subject of Church Renewal, some of them profound and some superficial. All are superficial whenever they propose surrender to our current naturalism and subjectivism, by giving up divine transcendence, and the incarnation and the possibility of real miracle. Christian leaders will not win the respect of a pagan society by accepting its ideas, while covering them with a veneer of Christian language. We must never forget Kierkegaard's warning about the danger which faces Christians whenever they cease to be in tension with the popular mentality. It is one of the surest insights of Robert Raines that the Church "is meant to be at tension with the customs and the traditions of every culture."[7]

We need not pay much attention to critics of the existent Church when they operate out of obvious hatred or when they have no alternatives to suggest. Mere diagnosis is too easy. But we can rightly pay attention to those who criticize the Church because they love her so deeply that they want her to achieve her true character. It is noticeable that the criticisms which probe most deeply are those which are conducted with affection; the best critics are those who stand on the inside. One example of this is provided by the brilliant pastor and professor of Ham-

[7] *New Life in the Church* (New York: Harper & Row, 1963), p. 17.

burg, Helmut Thielicke, in his call for renewal entitled *The Trouble with the Church*.[8]

The fact that the best critics are insiders, standing in marked contrast to those who merely throw stones, is not really hard to understand. The amazing truth is that God creates a community of saints out of sinful men and women. Those who are detached observers do not and cannot know this, but those who are really involved know it because they, themselves, are both saints and sinners. Close contact with a redeemed people makes us both weep and shout for joy, and do both at the same time.

What we need now is a true conversion, not merely of individuals, but of the Church itself. They are wholly mistaken who suppose that this means the rejection of our basic theology. What is needed, instead, is an understanding of how the Church may become the vehicle for the expression of the basic theology already known. Indeed, one of our important steps is to begin to realize how exceedingly revolutionary the primary Christian convictions really are. If God *is,* if He is like Christ, and if each human being is made in His image, we have a world view more revolutionary than Marxism or any other system which claims to be able to change the world. The trouble lies not in the theology, but in our failure to comprehend its dynamic qualities.

If the central Christian convictions are accepted seriously, every major human enterprise takes on new excitement. The work of the scientist is ennobled and his motivation heightened because, though he is a poor finite creature, he is seeking to deal with divine truth and to think a few of God's thoughts after Him. The social worker, if he is a committed Christian, is not merely holding down a job, or working the will of a political machine; he is seeking to bring emancipation to human beings who were made to be God's partners in creation. Each poor confused person, whose life is marked by failure and frustration, is seen in a wholly new light when viewed from the Christian perspective. No longer is he merely a cog in the industrial machine nor is he an incidental figure in the class struggle, because he is intrinsically precious. He is precious, not because of his

[8] Translated by John W. Doberstein (New York: Harper & Row. 1965).

achievement, which may be essentially nil, but rather because of his derivation and his potential destiny. He is potentially a member of the Kingdom of Christ. And it is the King, we must remember, who says, "Truly, I say to you, as you did it to one of the least of these my brethren, you did it to me" (Matt. 25:40).

The renewal of the Church will be in progress when it is seen as a fellowship of consciously inadequate persons who gather because they are weak, and scatter to serve because their unity with one another and with Christ has made them bold. This is the only kind of Christianity that can stand up to the challenge of the militant paganism and the fanaticism of the New Left. It will win, in the long run, because it is more revolutionary than they are.

Often, in the past, the Church has failed because, though it has realized the necessity of distinction from the world, it has fastened upon distinctions which are essentially trivial. We can see now, for example, that the "plain garb" of eighteenth-century Quakers was fundamentally a mistake in Christian strategy. The wearers who exhibited their distinctive marks were making real sacrifices, because they did not wish to seem different from their neighbors. It is important to realize that they adopted plainness of speech and apparel, not as a whim, but as a witness against the superficial fashions of the uncommitted. But the practice was, in spite of high motives, a mistaken one, and it was mistaken because it called attention to differences which were small rather than to big ones.

Another familiar example of distinctiveness is that of the rejection of jewelry and cosmetics on the part of certain American sects, early in the twentieth century. This was true especially of the Free Methodists and the Nazarenes. Only a very insensitive outsider could fail to be moved by the spirit in which such sacrifices were undertaken. It is still moving to read of good women taking off their wedding rings and placing them in the offering plates. Those who ridicule such actions are telling more about themselves than about the objects of their ridicule. The religion of the early Nazarenes, whatever else it may have been, was not mild religion. And many of the good effects are noticeable to this day. The mistake of such actions is not the mistake of being willing to be a conscious minority, but rather the mistake of arriving at distinctiveness too simply.

What marks are there which are really distinctive, but not trivial? There may be many such, but one is the combination of personal austerity and imaginative compassion. The persons who accept this mark will, on the one hand, reject the popular standard of conspicuous personal expenditure. They will not seek to impress others by the amount which they are able to spend upon their own comfort or entertainment. In short, they will be marked by a general spirit of simplicity, and in this they will be more tough with themselves than they are with others. They will accept a discipline, both of time and of money, which is the opposite of easy self-indulgence. On the other hand, they will use their energy and their money, which represent accumulated energy, to help other people who have no claim upon them except that they are human beings whom God loves.

The compassion which should be the chief external mark of a committed Christian minority may well begin with the relations to fellow members in the redemptive society, but must not be limited to them. "It is our care for the helpless," wrote Tertullian, "our practice of loving-kindness, that brands us in the eyes of many of our opponents." It is not to be concluded from this testimony that the Christians of Tertullian's day had any monopoly on such practical compassion, since there were undoubtedly non-Christian individuals who exhibited similar characteristics. The point is that, among committed Christians, the compassion was so general that it could be noticed by outsiders. The love of Christ made a visible difference in the love of men. Christians are not the only ones who have been pioneers in social progress, but the Christian record is really very impressive. The work for the care of the insane and the work in prison reform, both arising largely from Christian conviction, are essential features of Western civilization. The deepest mark of committed Christianity is the difference it makes.

The original miracle of the Church is one which never ceases to impress the thoughtful student. Certainly there can be no

Christianity without it, for mere individual religiousness soon comes to nothing. What is amazing is that Christ's impact on the world was perpetuated by such inadequate people as the original Apostles and the men and women of Corinth to whom the Apostle Paul wrote deathless prose and poetry. According to our common proverb, a chain is no stronger than its weakest link. The aphorism may be true, when applied strictly to the realm of the mechanical, but it is absurdly untrue when applied to a social organism such as the Church of Jesus Christ. All the links were weak, yet the chain survived! Ignorant men, united in Christ, produced a kind of wisdom. This is clearly miraculous, but it ought not to be rejected for that reason, since miracle is intrinsic to the Gospel.

Some knowledge of Church history is a source of encouragement, for renewal has often come in the darkest periods. However virulent some of the attacks on the Gospel may be today, they cannot equal those which were standard in the early part of the eighteenth century. Bishop Joseph Butler, in the Advertisement, prefixed to the first edition of *The Analogy of Religion* and dated 1736, wrote:

It has come, I know not how, to be taken for granted, by many persons, that Christianity is not so much as a subject of inquiry; but that it is, now at length, discovered to be fictitious. And accordingly they treat it, as if, in the present age, this were an agreed point among all people of discernment; and nothing remained, but to set it up as a principal subject of mirth and ridicule, as it were by way of reprisals, for its having so long interrupted the pleasures of the world.

It was after this that the miracle of the Wesleyan revival came.

Our hope today depends upon the renewal of the miracle. Though we know this, we are still puzzled about the way to proceed. The miracle is the work of God Almighty, but poor creatures like ourselves may be used by God to provide some of the conditions of the new life that must emerge. The following chapters are one effort to clarify the conditions of renewal.

CHAPTER 2

A Practical Starting Point

Perplexity comes to us simply and solely because we are min-isters.

—Karl Barth

Any great task is difficult, but it is especially difficult to know how to begin. We know that the world needs the Christian faith as a redemptive force; we know that this force is inoperative except through the Church; we know that the Church requires reconstruction; but how is it to be done? Clearly, we cannot begin everywhere at once; we need a usable handle with which to start the operation. We must find something that is a manageable unit, of which we can take hold. What is it?

The more we ponder this practical question the more clear it is that the practical starting point is the ministry, though this does not mean that the ministry is everything. The whole conception of the ministry is perplexing, partly because the term "ministry," as used in the modern world, is highly ambiguous. There is a deep ineptitude in equating the terms "clergy" and "church-man," not wholly different from the ineptitude of equating "the religious" with those who have adopted the discipline and garb of a separate order. In the ideal sense, all Christians are minis-ters, but for practical purposes this is not true. Those who think of themselves as ministers, whether lay or professional, are people who may be assumed to have a degree of dedication which makes the beginning of renewal possible. Ministers are important be-

34

cause, both potentially and actually, they are multipliers. If we can reach these people with a new vision of the Church, we can consequently reach others through them. The ministry is the point at which to begin because ministers are usually placed where they can make a difference.

The problem is that of how a minority can be effective in the world or can even survive. Being a minority by no means insures survival, though it is certainly not an absolute barrier to survival. The minority will not be effective unless it knows that it *is* a minority and is blessed with a powerful leadership. Though it seems strange that it should be so, it is a fact that one man, rightly placed in the ministry, can make an enormous difference in the lives of other men and in the total impact of the Church on the world.

There are many historical examples of the effect which one man can have in the life of a local congregation. Eli Lilly, in his history of Christ Church, Indianapolis, has come to the rather surprising conclusion that, in all the ups and downs of vitality, the difference arises primarily, not from external forces, but from the quality of leadership. Here is his measured conclusion: "The thoughtful study of Christ Church history since its establishment shows one outstanding revelation. Leadership is the pearl without price."[1] Mr. Lilly discovered that, among eighteen rectors in one hundred and nineteen years, only five had inspired an upsurge of life. His reasoned judgment is that unless we can get good men and unless we can re-educate the ones whom we have, we shall languish, whatever our budgets or our buildings may be.

Among the other careful observers who share Mr. Lilly's important conclusion is Douglas Horton. "The older I grow," writes Dr. Horton, "the more clearly I see that leadership is basic. Time and again we have witnessed in a church a change for the better or for worse with the coming of a new minister. Given the same people, the same social environment, the same instruments

[1] *The Little Church on the Circle* (Indianapolis: Christ Protestant Episcopal Church, 1957), p. 321.

to work with, one man will discover to the church its real reason for being and uncap latent forces of great spiritual power while the other will fail."[2]

Sometimes a man is able to multiply his spirit in the lives of others in a congregation even after his death or his departure to another place. A vivid illustration of continuing effect is that of Clark Poling, who died as a chaplain on the North Atlantic while on leave from his pastorate at the Reformed Church of Schenectady, New York. Though it has now been many years since Clark Poling died, the visitor to the remarkable congregation which he once served is still able to sense his continuing influence upon the lives of the members.

The pastor is important, not because he is wiser or better than are other men, but because he is so placed that he may be able to draw out and direct the powers of other men. All of his effectiveness is in the changed lives of other persons. Though there are some structures to guide him, the chief element is his own vision of himself and what his work might be.

It is not fair to stress the potential importance of the professional ministry without also stressing, at the same time, the vast perplexity which many pastors feel at this particular juncture in history. Because they want someone to listen, and because my address is easy to find, I receive a constant stream of letters from clergymen who are so frustrated in their work that they desire some kind of change in vocation. Some say that they are placed in impossible situations; others say they hate the image which seems to be forced upon them; nearly all wonder if they would be more effective to leave the pastorate and engage in some secular occupation. While the alternative tasks most often proposed are those of college teaching and social work, a good many say that they are about ready to go into business and thus to identify themselves wholly with the secular world. One insurance company now employs more than a hundred former pastors.

The decision of so many professional ministers to find other

[2] "The Idea of a Theological Seminary," *The Hartford Quarterly* (Summer, 1963), p. 7.

employment, combined with the much-publicized shortage of students who apply for entrance to the theological seminaries, produces a really urgent problem. That the problem is general and is by no means limited to old-line Protestants is shown by Cardinal Cushing's report about dropouts from Roman Catholic seminaries. Though there was a time when the archdiocese of Boston graduated seventy priests a year, the most recent report from St. John's Seminary listed only thirty-one graduates. There is no escape from the conclusion that the professional ministry is not as attractive as it once was, and that it is difficult to attract the ablest men. There is no real chance of Church Renewal unless this problem is solved. In recent years we have stressed the lay or universal ministry, and this we should have done, but, with no conflict of interest whatever, we need now to stress the professional ministry because, without the right leadership, the powers of the lay ministry will not be recognized and developed. The lay ministry is a great idea, but it will not do itself; it will not emerge in power unless it is consciously and deliberately encouraged, and it will not be encouraged unless there are able pastors and teachers to perform this liberating task.[3]

More and more the problem is that of image. The professional ministers, especially when they are persons of outstanding integrity, as many are, simply cannot accept the mold into which they are supposed to be cast. The best mind hates to be looked upon as the official pray-er at all ceremonial occasions. Partly the revulsion arises from the fact that such a task is too easy, for it is not difficult to learn a few clichés and to adopt the right tone. The amazing fact is that this satisfies so many, though the honest clergyman is quick to realize that such a performance makes practically no difference at all in the structure of civilization. A school can get a man ready for ceremonial tasks without much effort. Several of my correspondents fear that this is what has happened to

[3] The first clear voice in the twentieth century, which expressed the idea that there were undeveloped powers among laymen, was apparently that of John R. Mott. His impact was made, near the end of the first third of our century, in a book entitled *Liberating the Lay Forces of Christianity* (New York: The Macmillan Company, 1932).

them. "As a recent theological seminary graduate," writes one young man, "I am burdened with the feeling that I am the finished product of a factory for ministers. This is not a good feeling."

Part of the problem, by a curious paradox, is the very respect in which the professional ministry is held. The clergyman is still able to avail himself of personal privileges if he will. These range from free tickets at church dinners to the cancellation of parking or speeding fines. In New York a man wearing a clerical collar is often told by the bus drivers not to pay for transportation, and one prominent New York clergyman reports that he believes that it is impossible for a man in clerical garb to be arrested in his city. Though some men thrive on such special privileges, the best men tend to resent them bitterly. They do not want to be kept chaplains or professional holy men. They may not be entirely clear about the image of the ministry which would be acceptable to them, but they are very clear about what it is which they hate. They writhe when, at a dinner for Christian men, all of whom ought to be expected to be able to pray publicly, the pastor is, almost without exception, asked to say Grace. By superhuman effort a man may break out of this mold, but there is no doubt that it is the one which great numbers of lay members expect of their pastors. Because the recruitment of the strongest leaders is absolutely necessary for the effectiveness of the Church in the contemporary world, the urgent task is that of producing a new image of religious leadership which will be sufficient to enlist the interest of such men. Unless the image of expectation is altered, we must expect further decline and even decay.

As is true when facing other deep problems in Christian strategy, we are helped by a new look at the New Testament model. This is not to say that we can understand perfectly the character of Christian leadership as it existed in the first century or that there is a fixed pattern to which we should return, with no possibility of growth and progress, but it is to say that we shall be wise to try to see what was occurring in the period when the Gospel exhibited its greatest vitality, against odds greater than

our own. How did they do it? The right approach of the modern
Christian, when he faces the New Testament, is a combination of
humility and wonder. There, if anywhere, we may learn how to
operate as an effective minority with many adversaries.

One of the most striking aspects of the earliest Christianity was
the almost total eclipse of the priestly side of Old Testament
religion. Though most of the first Christians were Jews, and
though they held their Jewish heritage in high esteem, they neglected the priests in the Temple. In the Gospel record, Christ
seems to have paid almost no attention to these priests who were
so numerous that they had a platoon system of rotation in their
ceremonial duties. Very early Christians began to use the word
"minister," which is the equivalent of "servant," but nowhere in
the New Testament or in other early Christian literature is the
word *hierus,* "priest," employed as the equivalent of the Christian ministry.

As Robert Barclay saw in the seventeenth century, the conventional modern distinction between the clergy and laity simply
does not occur in the New Testament at all.[4] The word "minister" is not, in New Testament usage, the designation of a professional holy man at all, but may be applied to anyone who ministers, regardless of the secular mode of employment. That the
tentmakers, Aquila and Priscilla, mentioned in three different
books of the New Testament, were regarded as ministers there is
no doubt, but the contrast between this man and this woman
and the official Jewish priests is almost as great as can be imag-
ined.

The more we study the early Church the more we realize that
it was a society of ministers. About the only similarity between
the Church at Corinth and a contemporary congregation, either
Roman Catholic or Protestant, is that both are marked, to a great
degree, by the presence of sinners. After that the similarity ends,
for we think it is normal for one man to do all the preaching,
while the others are audience, whereas, in Corinth, many did the
preaching. "When you come together," reported their most

---

[4] *Apology for the True Christian Divinity,* Proposition **X, xxvi.**

famous visitor, "each one has a hymn, a lesson, a revelation, a tongue, or an interpretation" (I Cor. 14:26).

The ministry of original Christianity was one of its most revolutionary aspects. In contrast to all previous models, the new fellowship emerged as a dynamic force without *priest* or *rabbi* or *medicine man*. Since the one form of leadership which was retained, glorified and universalized was the prophetic one, the pattern, both in terms of what it included and what it excluded, was essentially new. The Gospel, so far as the history of religion is concerned, represented the emergence of genuine novelty, the emerging pattern rejecting both the lay and the clerical ideal. Though Christians accepted the necessity of leadership, the actual leadership was not sacerdotal. This explains, in some measure, why the new faith was so mystifying to observers, whether Jew or Greek; it did not conform to any known pattern of religious behavior. Thus there is no real surprise in the fact that the observers were sufficiently puzzled to say, "You bring some strange things to our ears" (Acts 17:20).

There is always a temptation to suppose that the early Christian emphasis required then or requires now a denial of differences in function. Why not say that all Christians are supposed to be ministers and leave it at that? Why not deny the need of pastors at all? The earliest Christians were far too realistic to fall into this trap, because they saw that, if the ideal of universal ministry is to be approximated at all, there must be some people who are working at the job of bringing this highly desirable result to pass. The disciples had the word of Christ about the necessity of laborers, if the harvest was to be rightly handled, and they knew that no grain harvests itself! According to the Gospel record, Christ twice commanded His followers to pray for the emergence of a labor force, which was the obvious bottleneck of the new movement. The harvest, i.e., the development of a redemptive fellowship made up wholly of ministers, is potentially great, but it cannot be actualized without the labor of men who are sufficiently gifted and dedicated to facilitate its accomplishment.

The New Testament pattern, then, involves, both a generalized and a particular ministry. When the Apostle Paul uses the term pastor he equates it with teacher and makes it very clear that this is by no means the whole conception of the ministry. The ministry is for all who are called to share in Christ's life, but the pastorate is for those who possess the peculiar gift of being able to help other men and women to practice any ministry to which they are called. The classic passage which, fortunately, is becoming more and more familiar to literate contemporary Christians, develops the pattern which we have come to call The Equipping Ministry. "And these were his gifts: some to be . . . pastors and teachers, to equip God's people for work in his service" (Eph. 4:12, NEB). The phrase "equipping ministry," as something which provides a new and more exciting image of what the professional ministry might be, has been stressed by several contemporary writers, particularly Robert Raines and Thomas Mullen.[5]

The idea of the pastor as the equipper is one which is full of promise, bringing back self-respect to men in the ministry when they are sorely discouraged by the conventional pattern. Here is a job which is as intrinsically hard, as the job of the official prayer at banquets is intrinsically easy. To watch for underdeveloped powers, to draw them out, to bring potency to actuality in human lives—this is a self-validating task. A man who knows that he is performing such a function is not bothered by problems of popular acceptance because he is working at something which he can respect. With self-respect he can bear the attacks of his enemies and detractors with a certain confidence. Though his life is not easy, he is saved from triviality, for he knows that his work is both necessary and important, because the stakes, so far as civilization is concerned, are high. Because the task is itself ennobling, he need not worry whether he is called "Reverend" or "Doctor." The dignity of his life is involved, not in status, but in function.

One of the ways by which the image of the professional minis-

---

[5] Robert Raines's book, which does this, is *New Life in the Church,* already mentioned in a previous footnote. Thomas Mullen's book is *The Renewal of the Ministry* (Nashville: Abingdon Press, 1963).

ter can be improved is that of a better linguistic designation. Language is often both a revelation of what men think and a barrier to improvement. To call a man who is engaged in the equipping ministry *the minister* of the congregation, as is now often done, is seen to be inept as soon as we examine the implication of such language. If Dr. Jones is *the* minister of the First Presbyterian Church of Centerville, it follows logically that the ordinary members are *not* ministers. And the shame is that this is exactly what many of them desire. It is clearly a neat device for people to hire someone to be their minister, thus relieving all of the ordinary members of ministerial responsibilities. But this way lies death, for there is no possibility of sustained or enlarged vitality without personal involvement, and personal involvement means ministry, if it means anything at all.

What then shall the equipper be called, if not the minister? Here we have real difficulty since all of the familiar terms have unacceptable overtones. "Elder" won't do for it sounds stuffy, and is as ridiculous when applied to a young man as is "Father" when applied to a bachelor. "Preacher," which was once conventional on the frontier, won't do for it refers to only one aspect, though an important one, of a complex function. In many ways "pastor" is best, partly because it is dignified by New Testament usage, but even more because it places emphasis upon the relationship to those who are being led. The Lutheran tradition has made zealous use of this term, with many good results, one of which is the avoidance of the temptation to make an indiscriminate and illicit use of the honorific "Doctor." In spite of these advantages, the word pastor implies much that we do not mean and ought not to mean. Sheep are not particularly productive, except in providing wool and mutton. Futhermore, sheep are notorious for their placidity while they are being led, but this is no part of the ideal of Christian men and women in the common ministry of common life. A man who supposes that his relationship to the members of a congregation is in any sense identical to the relationship between a shepherd and a flock is in for some big surprises. Another serious difficulty with pastoral terminology is that modern men have very little knowledge of the ways of sheep, some city dwellers never having seen a sheep in their whole lives. Here is a vivid example of how language can become almost meaningless because of a radical change in manner of living.

Some are now coming to believe that the least inadequate or distorting term for a spiritual leader in a congregation is "coach." This word has overtones which modern man comprehends very well, indeed. Furthermore, the image of the coach is one which can be universally honored by young and old alike. Everyone knows that, in the development of a football or a baseball team, the quality of the coaching staff often makes a crucial difference. With no essential change in the personnel of the players, the effectiveness of the team is sometimes changed radically when a new coach begins to operate. He sees that Smith can profitably be shifted from guard to halfback and that the fullback, having never been used in defense, may have in him the possibility of becoming a successful line-backer.

The glory of the coach is that of being the discoverer, the developer, and the trainer of the powers of other men. But this is exactly what we mean when we use the Biblical terminology about the equipping ministry. A Christian society is made up of men and women whose powers in the ministry are largely unused because they are unsuspected. The Christian coach will be one who is more concerned, therefore, in developing others than in enhancing his own prestige. Ideally, he will not do anything himself, if another can be enabled to grow by being encouraged to do it. If the sermon can be given effectively by an ordinary member, the pastor, in so far as he is truly a coach, may keep silent while the other speaks, even though the training of the other person may cost him far more in time and toil than his own preparation for speaking would have cost.

Since the equipping minister must not be above the heat of the battle, he is, ideally, not only a coach, but a "playing coach," sometimes carrying the ball himself and sometimes seeing to it that another carries it. Thus, he is both a minister and the encourager, a teacher and a developer of his fellow ministers, who are the members of the Church of Christ. The mark of his success is not the amount of attention which he can focus upon himself, but the redemptive character which emerges in the entire congregation or team. Fundamentally, he is called to be a catalytic agent, often making a radical difference while being relatively inconspicuous. This is a high ideal. Indeed, it is an ideal so high that it can be made attractive to the very men who are repelled by the lower ideal which is the only one which some of them have hitherto known. Such an ideal, if generally accepted, can provide a practical starting point for the reconstruction of the Church. It is not the end of the matter, but is undoubtedly a viable beginning.

As we seek the renewal of the Church as a redemptive agency in the world, we need to examine closely what the right function of a religious teacher in a local congregation should be. If a man is a coach, what are his proper duties? It is not hard to find plenty to do, but it is far from easy to know which duties should have priority, when there is inevitable conflict of demands. It is the clear recognition of the minority standing of the committed Christian society which gives us our best clue in making a reasonable answer to this urgent question. As the struggle gets harder the man who is liberated for professional Christian service must have in mind both the strengthening of the already committed and the reaching of the far larger body of the uncommitted. The task, whatever it may be, can never be single.

In the strengthening of the already committed, the liberated minister's first task is that of teacher. It is not an insignificant fact that pastor and teacher are equated in Ephesians 4:12. The people of the Church need careful teaching to keep them from falling away, under the constant pressures of the adversaries, but they need the teaching even more to equip them to become effective witnesses to the outside population. It is clear that the members must be the major witnesses, each one seeking to make a beneficent difference where he is, particularly in his daily work. The members of Christ's Kingdom are all meant to be ambassadors or even evangelists. The task of reaching the world is too great to be left merely to the pastors, however able they may be personally. But, if the members are to be effective ambassadors, they must be *taught*. That it is not easy to know how to make a witness is demonstrated by the ineptitude and failure of many who try, since goodwill is no substitute for skill in a task as important as this one. But who is to do the teaching? Obviously the only one who is trained for this task is the local pastor.

The notion that the professional minister's main job is that of the conduct of public worship is something which we must destroy if we are to get ready for a larger and more fruitful team ministry. In some areas the conduct of public worship is looked upon, not merely as the chief function, but as almost the sole function of a clergyman. We employ the vulgar phrase "occupying a pulpit," and in some congregations that is nearly all that the people desire. Consequently, they are not worried if a man is absent from the community nearly all of the hours of the week except one. This might suffice if religion were a ritualistic process, but true Christianity is not that kind of religion. We must understand that, whereas public worship is important, it is important only as the beginning of a total process. The matter of chief importance is the steady continuous ministry of all of the members, and the chief function of the pastor is to help people to get ready for this ministry. This cannot be done by a single twenty-five-minute sermon. People cannot normally learn without a teacher and good teaching is intrinsically an unhurried business. The congregation must, accordingly, be reconstructed into the pattern of a small theological seminary with the pastor as the professor.

What should the local theological professor teach? More than anything else, he should teach theology, i.e., the knowledge of God. This is to be done by the use of books, by the guidance of individual study, by organized discussions, and by lectures. The notion that theology is dull or necessarily abstruse is one which we must dispel as quickly as possible. Hard thinking about the nature of God, about the work of Christ, and about the vocation of the Christian is, of course, difficult, as is anything of importance, but it can be made exciting if the teacher is sufficiently disciplined in mind. The popular notion that theology is necessarily or normally a parade of long words must be dismissed as a device of the enemy. The equally popular notion that theology is dull must be attacked even more strongly, but this the good teacher can do by demonstration.

Unless we have a better study of theology in the Church there will be a disastrous falling away. Many members admit, when pressed, that they think that much of what the leaders of the Church are saying is not true and is said only as a kind of ritual. Thousands, who try to be good Christians, are deeply worried about the contrast between science and religion, convinced that scientific truths are verified, while religious truths are only affirmed. Nearly all of this problem could be solved by a better understanding of the impossibility of absolute proof, in science or anywhere else, and by a deeper conception of what the evidence for the basic Christian affirmation really is. Almost any thoughtful student can come to see that the alleged contrast between scientific certainty and religious wish-thinking is not what it is popularly supposed to be.

The best insurance against falling away is the development of a profound and well-grounded set of convictions. The good teacher can deal with the powerful cumulative evidence for the being of God; he can deal realistically with the difficulties of belief, such as those involved in the problem of evil; and he can show that survival after bodily death is more than a mere hope. Millions who are now church members have never engaged in any such study in all their lives. This is why they are such easy targets for the passing intellectual fads and also why they finally lose interest in the life of the Church. Ushering on Sundays and singing in the choir will not, in the long run, be substitutes for genuine conviction.

The purpose of teaching theology is not merely that of the confirmation of the faith of the members, in order to keep them from falling away. It is also preparation for their confrontation with questioning in the world. When a man on the production line is confronted by the doubts of a fellow worker whose wife is dying of cancer, it is not sufficient for him to say "Go to see my pastor." He must be ready to have a convincing answer when it is put, for that is the crucial time. "Always be prepared to make a defense to any one who calls you to account for the hope that is in you, yet do it with gentleness and reverence" (I Peter 3:15). One of the primary tasks of the Christian pastor is to engage in such teaching that the ordinary member, who is his theological student, can be effective when he is faced with the hard questions. Such teaching is never perfectly done, but it can be done in part, and some pastors do it amazingly well.

At the same time that a pastor is a teacher in the community, he must also be a scholar. That this follows necessarily from the recognition of minority status is obvious. Because every item of the Christian view of life is now under violent attack, the attack must be met. The people to meet it are the religious leaders who are liberated from secular earning in order to permit them to engage deeply in the struggle. Every day there are public attacks on the being of God, on the objectivity of the moral order, and on the value of the Church. If these attacks are not met, the battle is lost by default and the majority of Christians becomes utterly confused. The Christian must learn to outthink all opposition. That this is possible is demonstrated by the long history of the Christian faith which has met, in other centuries, attacks quite as strong as those encountered now. But thinking is hard work and we must have men who are prepared to engage in it.

One important consideration for the pastor as scholar is that concerning the vulnerability of all positions. If we are honest we freely admit that the Christian system involves difficulties, but so does every other system. No thoughtful person gives up a position merely because he discovers difficulties in it; he does not abandon it unless he is able to find other and alternative systems with *fewer* difficulties. One of the great things which I learned from my professors of philosophy at Johns Hopkins University was that, while philosophy might not provide me with a watertight intellectual defense of the Christian faith, it would, if used aright, help me to reveal the weakness of its enemies. By careful analysis it is possible to see that there are glaring weaknesses and *non sequiturs* in atheism, naturalism, positivism, scientism, and psychologism. The Christian must be a fighter, for he is always under attack, and his strongest method is that of attacking the attackers. The Church will not be as strong as it ought to be until each local pastor uses his precious freedom from outside employment in order to become a scholarly participant in the intellectual struggle of our day and generation.

In the recent past, which has been marked by both advance and decline in the life of the Church, one aspect of decline has involved preaching. A number of pastors have minimized preaching, claiming that they could be more effective if they were to stress only counseling or the leadership of discussion groups or the nurture of prayer groups. That these latter tasks are important needs to be said with insistence, but it does not follow that preaching dare be neglected. That this does not follow is one of the chief contributions of Helmut Thielicke, whose translator says categorically, "Wherever we find, even in this day, a vital, living congregation we find at its center vital preaching."[6] This is my impression, too. I think it likely that the men who derogate preaching are, for the most part, precisely those who cannot do it well. There have been no changes in our culture which alter the fact that the spoken word may be a powerful force in human life. Good preaching is still possible and sometimes it makes a crucial difference. Though the time when it was easy to assemble a crowd is over, at least for the immediate present, it is still true that people will gather where they have reason to believe that something will be said, with clarity and conviction, about life's most important issues.

Crowds may be hard to get in modern Germany, but they assemble in Hamburg to hear the preaching of Dr. Thielicke. They gather, in a similar fashion, in Edinburgh, to hear James S. Stewart. That is one reason for listening to Stewart's words when he speaks on the subject of preaching. "Do not listen," he says,.

[6] *The Trouble with the Church, op. cit.,* p. viii.

"to the foolish talk which suggests that, for this twentieth century, the preaching of the word is an anachronism, and that the pulpit, having served its purpose, must now be displaced. . . . As long as God sets his image on the soul, and men are restless till they rest in him, so long will the preacher's task persist, and his voice be heard through all the clamor of the world."[7]

One of the most courageous warnings provided by Dr. Thielicke is that against the tendency of the Church to escape into liturgism. This is something which we have all seen, but have not sufficiently deplored. There are pastors whose chief concern centers in the colors to be used in the chancel at different seasons of the year. One congregation has invested thirty thousand dollars in liturgical lighting effects. Thielicke sees this partly as a flight from preaching, suggesting that a preacher who can draw enough attention to his vestments may suppose that he can divert attention from the poverty of his thought.

Men are faced with a necessity—which is that the work of preaching is simply too hard for them—and they proceed to make a virtue of it by saying that their aim is to overcome subjectivity in the church. They foster a set order which must be performed according to the formulatory and the rubrics. Often this is accomplished by a great deal of solemn play-acting, dressing up in liturgical vestments, and wandering to and fro from the epistle side of the altar to the gospel side, from the altar to the lectern, pulpit and the sanctuary rail.[8]

One trouble with the liturgical approach is that it is too easy. The lines of the play can be learned fairly quickly and vestments can be donned without much intellectual effort, whereas effective preaching, directed to both mind and heart, comes only after much toil. Frequently the good sermon must grow in a man's mind for weeks before it reaches the form in which it can be rightly delivered. Usually, it changes radically during the period of its slow and painful growth. The emphasis on liturgical vestments may be pleasant for the tiny "core congregation" of those

[7] *Heralds of God* (New York: Charles Scribner's Sons, 1946).
[8] *Op. cit.*, p. 84.

who understand and consequently appreciate the subtle changes of liturgical style, but there is little likelihood that it will do anything at all for the alienated or perplexed masses who, whatever their failings, are seriously looking for something to overcome their intellectual and spiritual confusion. They are most likely to find this in the word fitly spoken. There is nothing wrong with trying to improve the form of public worship, and we all want to see things done decently and in order, but no pastor is worthy of his calling if he is primarily a worship expert.

It is important for the concerned pastor to know that many of the features, on which he lays stress, often do not touch the people of the congregation at all. Try inquiring of attenders to know what was said in the Responsive Reading or in the Scripture Lesson and you may be surprised to learn how little gets through to the average person. The forthrightness of Clyde Reid in recording his own experience in this connection is almost shocking. "I have never in my lifetime," he writes, "heard a single comment by a single parishioner on the content of a responsive reading."[9] Many admit that they shut their minds off completely and wait until the readings are completed, before they give attention again. This is particularly true of the conventional benedictions. Some, when questioned, say that the familiar benedictions are, for them, as much gibberish as would be the alphabet said backwards. One of the chief lessons learned by those of us who were students forty years ago, when Studdert-Kennedy spoke so powerfully to American student audiences, was his freshness of approach in creating and employing benedictions which people did hear, because they were at once unconventional and vividly relevant. People who will not even hear Hebrews 13:20, 21,[10] when used as a benediction, because it is like an old coin rubbed smooth by much handling, may pay startled attention if the preacher ends by saying:

[9] *The God-Evaders* (New York: Harper & Row, 1966), p. 56.
[10] "Now may the God of peace who brought again from the dead our Lord Jesus, the great shepherd of the sheep, by the blood of the eternal covenant, equip you with everything good that you may do his will, working in you that which is pleasing in his sight, through Jesus Christ; to whom be glory for ever and ever. Amen."

> Go in joy;
> Sin no more;
> Love God.
> Serve His children.

What the professional minister needs to face continually is the sobering fact that he does no good if he is not heard. And hearing is much more than the mere possession of ears. All great tasks, such as those of physicians and lawmakers, require unrelenting imaginative attention, but there is no task in the world which is more demanding in this regard than is the task of the servant of a Christian congregation. Certainly it is not a task for the lazy or the easygoing, whose desire is to have a comfortable life. God never gave any man enough brains to do the job adequately, but there are some men who have done it well enough to make those of us who have profited from their labors eternally grateful.

We cannot talk adequately about the reconstruction of the ministry, as a starting point for Church Renewal, without careful consideration of what is ordinarily called the lay ministry. This is admittedly a poor term, but it may be less confusing than is any known alternative. By it we mean the ministry in daily life of mothers and clerks and factory workers and professional people, who have two vocations, one of which is that of representing Jesus Christ. Some of us have given thought to how such a ministry of common life should be performed, but we know that we have not done more than to scratch the surface of the problem.

The misunderstandings about the lay ministry are numerous. For example, one woman writes that it is a surprise to her to learn that the lay ministry has something to do with ordinary toil. She had always supposed, she said, that it was merely a matter of laymen reading the Scripture in the period of worship on Sunday morning. Others run the risk of supposing that the purpose in the lay revolution is to make engineers and lawyers into pseudo-clergy, performing little tasks about the church building, as the pastor's unpaid helpers.

Though there is great merit in using lay members in the conduct of worship, because anything is better than a one-man show, and also because we cannot approach the New Testament pattern unless something of this nature is essayed, we must go on to say that the use of lay ministers is far from foolproof. It is good to have ordinary members pray publicly, but, if they are to do so, they need to be *taught*. The salesman who prays publicly can be even more cliché ridden and verbose than is the clergyman. There is no real advantage in producing a new class of the semi-professionals. This is one reason why it is a distinct gain, when laymen read the Scriptures, to allow them to sit in the nave, with their families, to walk to the lectern to read, and then return to their original places. When such men sit in the chancel they tend to appear to be semiprofessionals, in which case the sharpness of the impact is lost. The greatest advantage of having the participating laymen sit in the body of the congregation is that such a practice helps to break the stereotype of a performance in which one class is that of the actors and the other class is that of the auditors.

However valuable the participation of laymen in public worship may be, it must be clearly understood that such is never the lay member's chief ministry. In the nature of the case, his chief witness must be given outside the place of worship, for the vineyard, where laborers are needed, is not located in the church building. It is located most often in factories and offices and clubs.

The old-fashioned idea was that the pastor had a program, and that the members were his helpers in putting his program into effect. Thus, it has long been understood that lay members have a function, but it has often been seen as little more than an auxiliary function. Women, it has been thought, could be very useful in preparing church suppers or in working with the altar guild, while men could look after the repairs of the building, take up the offering, guide the work of the janitor, and help in the every-member canvass. But the main show was the pastor's; he was the entrepreneur; the Church was his business; and if he were not careful he would refer to the Church as his.

Now, with the new emphasis on what the Church might be in the world, the familiar picture is entirely reversed. At last we are beginning to see that it is the ordinary member who has a program and that the pastor is *his* helper. The lay Christian, who takes his calling seriously, is eager to make an impact for Christ upon the world in which he lives and works, but how is he to do it? While no one wholly knows the answer, the poor people whom God has called to this ministry may help each other by pooling their inadequate insights. Such is the main point of a small group of Christians who gather regularly to pray, to study, and to share each other's problems. Nearly always something comes out of the fellowship which makes a difference, for new ideas, like new lives, are normally conceived in conjunction.

Valuable as the assistance of the small group may be, nothing can take the place of the dedicated pastor who is the modest helper of the members. He is humble enough to know that those engaged in business are operating on the front lines, while he is in the rear echelons. But those in the rear echelons are also valuable. The good Christian coach may give important advice, for instance, to a committed man who is the principal of a public high school and who wonders what he can do or should do. How far, for instance, should he go in arranging consciously Christian convocations in Holy Week? To what degree is he hampered by the fact that the Supreme Court has ruled that the state must be neutral in matters of religion? Should he go on boldly and plan a religious baccalaureate service for the graduates as was formerly done? Because these are not easy questions, the individual Christian ought not to be left to handle them alone. He needs both the help of the dedicated group and the help of the dedicated religious leader. It is easy to think of other problems, in some ways similar and in some ways different, involved in the performance of almost every secular occupation.

There is no possibility of an effective Church unless it includes a pastoral system, but this must never be construed as a system with a single pastor. The magic lies, neither in the emphasis upon laymen alone, nor upon professionals alone, but in the creative combination. Actually, each member is called to be a pastor to somebody, because each stands where someone asks questions which demand answers. The trouble with the ordinary pastoral system is not that it goes too far, but that it does not go far enough. *There can be no vital Church without a multipastoral system!*

When we think how difficult the ministry, whether lay or professional, really is, we wonder at the temerity of anyone who is willing to undertake it. The days are never long enough, and there is no discharge in the war. But the ministry, in all its aspects, is the very stuff of the Christian religion. Christianity is a religion for those who know that they are servants, because they are enlisted in the troops of their Servant Lord.

CHAPTER 3

Conditions of Emergence

The readiness is all.
—William Shakespeare

It is wholly possible that, just as there is a "hedonistic paradox," there is also a "renewal paradox." Perhaps renewal, like happiness, being always a by-product, can never be achieved by direct seeking. Men, being only creatures, do not create life, though they may have, as gardeners or husbandmen, the privilege of sharing in creation to the extent that they can guide, nourish, and prune. It is good for us to recognize our limitations. We can make wonderful roads, but we have not been able to eliminate either poverty or war. We have developed marvelous science, but we are not equally successful in the personal relationships between individual scientists. The self cannot integrate itself, though it may *be* integrated by commitment to a point of reference outside the self.

The new life which we so sorely need, either in the individual Christian or in the fellowship which we call the Church, is something which we cannot produce at will, but we do have the modest function of meeting some of the conditions of its emergence. The conditions of renewal are clearly more demanding than has been generally recognized. To build a new building today is a costly undertaking, but the rebuilding of a genuine Christian fellowship is far more costly. It cannot be done either by a new set of gadgets or by the rearrangement of the lives of uncommitted people. Nor can it be done by pronouncements for publication in the press. For example, the most renewed congregation in regard to racial justice may be one which, while it makes no pronouncements at all, affects, through its members who are Christian merchants and policemen and judges, a higher standard of personal dignity for all and a closer approximation to equality of justice. Genuine renewal sometimes receives the least publicity. The important test of the life of the Church is that of the difference which is being made in the daily lives of its members, who constitute the Church.

The most obvious condition of renewal is repentance, because there is no other way of being sufficiently dissatisfied with what we have come to accept as standard behavior. Ten years ago, when the discussion of renewal was in its earlier stages, Dr. Visser 't Hooft, then General Secretary of the World Council of Churches, wrote, "All great renewals in the history of the Church have been movements of *repentance*. This is inevitable because renewal presupposes a break with the old world."[1] It is impressive to recognize that the note of repentance is common to the teaching both of John the Baptist and of Christ, that it is found throughout the New Testament, and that it is expressed in the first of the famous theses which Martin Luther nailed to the Church door at Wittenberg, when a radical change was required. Repentance is the most insistent note in the *Private Prayers* of Lancelot Andrewes.[2]

Every genuine return to the Bible seems to open the door to renewal. On the surface this appears to be strange and is certain to be resisted by those who suppose that they are sophisticated, but there is really no denying the fact. Much of the new life associated with Luther's powerful ministry was the direct result of the general encounter with the Biblical record. Even George Fox, who sought to draw men to acquaintance with Christ in the

[1] *The Renewal of the Church* (Philadelphia: The Westminster Press, 1956), p. 95.
[2] The central prayer of Andrewes was "Give me a molten heart." "I can sin much," he wrote, "I cannot repent much." In examining his own life he wrote, "I need more grief."

living present, was clearly inspired by the Scriptures and was said to know most of its passages by heart. Why should an ancient book make such a difference after hundreds of years? No contemporary thinker has answered this question better than has Dr. Visser 't Hooft. "The Bible," he says, "is the authentic record of the only radically new event that has ever taken place in the world."[3]

Christians, if renewal of the Church is to come, must engage in hard and clear thinking. In short, one of the most important steps in readiness is *theological*. Perhaps we are already past the time when "theology" was a bad word, even in the Church. We hope so! We dare not neglect theological thinking for the clear reason that theology cannot be avoided. Since there is no such thing as "no theology," the only alternative to a valid theology is a poor or confused one. Men, so long as they are truly human, are bound to deal with the ultimate questions, but it is blasphemous to deal with these by slogans and catchwords and clichés.

We certainly need to repent of our poor contemporary theology. The amazing thing is that hundreds of thousands of copies of the most confused books have been purchased. This is, however, some indication of the hunger. The cliché "God is not a Person," has been published and republished, not merely by avowed atheists, whom we might honor for their sincerity, but by supposed Christian leaders. What all of the representatives of this theological fad seem to miss is that, if they are right, then Christ was wrong. Christ clearly addressed the Father as a Person, especially in the haunting personal prayer, "I thank thee, Father, Lord of heaven and earth" (Matt. 11:25, Luke 10:21). We need not subscribe to the linguistic conception of philosophy in order to see that a person is the only being that can be addressed reasonably as "Thou."

We have had a spate of books which try to tell the reader that God is not "a being," but only the Ground of Being. It is time to say clearly, that there is no wonder in the fact that such a denial of divine existence is confusing to the lay Christian, for it *is*

[3] *Op. cit.*, p. 92.

confused. The only logical alternative to existence is nonexistence! If God is not really a *Being* then He is merely a projection of our feeble minds and Freud was right. It is one of the merits of the Roman Catholic theologians, particularly those deeply influenced by St. Thomas Aquinas, that they have not been taken in by the self-styled new theology. They have attacked it, not because it is new, but because it is confused. The confusion on the problem of existence has been brilliantly exposed by Jacques Maritain in *Approaches to God*.[4]

We cannot have an adequate theology unless it is rigorously examined. The popular alternative to rigor is the following of a fad, with more emotion than criticism. We have experienced such a fad in the uncritical acceptance of everything written by the martyr, Dietrich Bonhoeffer, even in the days immediately prior to his tragic murder, when he was obviously under strain and with no opportunity for revision. It is not fair to a man, especially to one who has suffered and who is not available for reply, to take his sentences out of context and to treat them as inspired. John W. Doberstein has provided a needed warning by saying, "The fact is that Bonhoeffer would squirm to read what these theologians, and even bishops, have extrapolated from a few tentative and private ruminations in his prison cell."[5]

One of our most serious theological dangers in the recent past has been the tendency to concede too much to the enemy. There are writers who are so eager to reach the minds of the cultured despisers that they water down the Christian faith in order to make it palatable. This is called adjustment, but it runs the risk of surrender, and then nothing is accomplished. If the Christian thinker, in his admirable effort to be understood by those outside the faith, ends by saying essentially what the enemies of Christ are already saying, nothing is accomplished. This is what occurs when we give up the Incarnation or the uniqueness of Christ or the authority of the Scriptures or the objective efficacy of prayer. We are not doing the positivist any good if we merely accept his

[4] New York: Collier Books, 1962.
[5] Translator's note to Thielicke, *The Trouble with the Church, op. cit.*, p. ix.

position and join his camp, while still claiming, somehow, to be in the Church. Any theology which is not a direct challenge to the assumptions of the philosophical naturalist is not worth elucidating.

The Christian must always be sufficiently humble to accept any truth which is scientifically validated, but he will, at the same time, have enough intellectual sophistication to know that such validation is never simple. The Christian, who understands his position, will modestly admit that absolute proof of God's existence is not possible, but he will also be wise enough to know that there is likewise no absolute proof in science or anywhere else. The path to follow is one in which we accept the weight of evidence whenever it appears, but always with a reverent skepticism. Thus, the weight of evidence is now strong enough to lead to the conclusion that the earth is millions of years old and that other forms of life appeared long before the advent of *Homo sapiens*. The Christian sees no problem in this, because he thinks that all true science is a belated discovery of God's truth and is inspired by Him.

There is a world of difference between the humble acceptance of scientifically verified conclusions about particular occurrences and the acceptance of the dogmas of positivism, which is, in reality, a position in philosophy rather than one in science. The upholder of determinism, we must note, has gone far beyond any scientific conclusion, when he adopts a faith which is radically incompatible with any acceptance of moral responsibility. There is no reason at all why the Christian, who holds a much less limited faith, and is consequently more "broad-minded," should adopt such a position, however fashionable it may be. The Archbishop of Canterbury, in a recent set of lectures, has touched briefly upon this important point of Christian intellectual strategy. He warns against giving up a Christian doctrine merely because "modern man does not like or understand" it. He recognizes the danger of employing "wrong kinds of plea that Christianity may be made acceptable."[6] It would be a sad paradox if

[6] Arthur Michael Ramsey, *Sacred and Secular* (New York: Harper & Row, 1965), p. 73.

the Christian faith should be damaged more by its exponents than by its enemies. What we need is to be sufficiently critical to realize that not all of the supposed steps in renewal are helpful. This is part of what is meant by being as wise as serpents.

Fortunately, in our needed effort to engage in tough theological thinking, for which so many are evidently hungry, we have valuable resources upon which we can depend. One of the finest of intellectual resources is the work of the late William Temple, whose monumental work *Nature, Man and God* has stood the test of time and criticism, so that it has far more contemporary relevance than do many of the works written more recently.[7] Temple understood the totality of the Gospel, seeing that it must be both social and individual; he welcomed the insights of natural scientists, seeing them reverently as part of God's revelation; he rejected all small conceptions of God and saw that nothing less than the concept of the Infinite Person was large enough to meet the requirements of critical thought; he accepted gladly the work of Biblical criticism yet, at the same time, his greatest strength lay in the perusal of the Biblical narrative, particularly that of the Gospel of St. John.

In singling out William Temple, it is not implied that he stands alone, for there are many on whom we can depend with confidence. Our attitude toward such thinkers may reasonably be that of profound gratitude. Because the ordinary Christian faces a difficult task in trying to solve the hard problems of faith, and to answer the attacks of his unbelieving neighbors, he can be extremely grateful for the fact that there are men who have already engaged in the arduous task of trying to express a faith which is consistent both with itself and with the facts of the world as known. Every intelligent Christian tries to be orthodox, in that he aspires to engage in sound thinking, and to avoid heresy. Part of his discipline is to become sufficiently sensitive to realize that many modern ideas, touted for their novelty, are in

[7] The contemporary failure to recognize Temple's greatness is pathetic. For example, Walter Kaufmann, in his ambitious *Religion from Tolstoy to Camus,* does not even include Temple's work, though he includes the works of many lesser men.

reality ancient heresies, long ago exposed because of their inner contradictions.

We cannot emphasize too strongly the necessity of clear Christian thinking. Beautiful sanctuaries, paved parking lots, and new liturgies will do very little for people who sit in worship with their fingers crossed and do not really believe the faith which is expounded. Often the layman dismisses what the preacher says as something irrelevant to his situation and generation. When he joins a group where he is no longer afraid to be frank, the supposedly faithful member often admits that he has never really accepted what he thinks he has heard. He has, for example, grave reservations about the idea of *creation*. Did not the world evolve of itself? Do we really need the hypothesis of Infinite Purpose to make sense of the physical, biological, and psychological development? These questions seldom come to the surface when the Church provides merely a one-way preaching. There is little chance of renewal if all that we have is the arrangement by which one speaks and the others listen. One trouble with this conventional system is that the speaker never knows what the unanswered questions are, or what reservations remain in the layman's mentality.

Somehow or other we must arrange opportunities for Christian dialogue, since the old idea of the preacher standing ten feet above contradiction simply will not do, even for *him*. The practice in some congregations of worshiping on Sunday morning from ten to eleven, with opportunity of intellectual encounter between speaker and listeners from eleven to twelve, is one practical way of uncovering and facing difficulties, but there may be others which are equally good. What is important is for the Christian leaders to know that the defense of the faith has not been as convincing as they have supposed it to be.

There is little doubt that one of the best evidences of vitality in the contemporary Church has been that of vigorous activity in pressing for moral improvement in our culture. There has been, at least on the part of a minority of Christians, a true dedication to the redress of social wrongs and the overcoming of injustice, which has appeared more vividly on the racial front than anywhere else. Indeed, for some in our time the struggle against racial justice has produced a fierce dedication not unlike that of our ancestors who found the meaning of their lives in the struggle against slavery. Controversial as many actions have been, there is little doubt that social action of this kind has made the Church seem relevant, even to some of its cultured despisers. Martin Luther King is not easily dismissed.

Though the major greatness of the Church in our generation has been ethical rather than theological, it is important to point out that the ethical drive cannot be maintained or rightly guided if it is divorced from theological presuppositions. Apart from a close adherence to Christ and repeated reference to His revelation, even the effort to fight injustice may become bitter and unloving. Only the naïve can suppose that, because the protester goes limp, he is therefore loving.

One of the clearest warnings against the supposed sufficiency of an untheological ethics was voiced by Richard Niebuhr, whose words are especially worthy of attention because he was, himself, devoted to the ethical application of the Gospel. His vivid dictum was "that ethical solutions depend quite as much on theological understanding as vice versa. Questions about divine and human nature, about God's action and man's, arise at every point, as the radical Christian undertakes to separate himself from the cultural society, and as he engages in debate with members of other Christian groups."[8] The strongest reason for racial justice is a doctrine, and the doctrine is concerned with creation. The further we go, the more we see the profundity of Chesterton's remark that even democracy makes no sense apart from the dogma of the divine creation of man.

One major spot in which the lay Christian needs help is in having answers to the constant attacks which are bound to come to him, even more than they come to the clergyman. Because, when he is alone and therefore without help, some objections sound unanswerable, the layman is certainly put on the defen-

[8] H. Richard Niebuhr, *Christ and Culture* (New York: Harper & Row, Torchbook, 1951), p. 76

sive. We shall make a great step forward when we help him to move over to the position of attack. What he needs to know, and what he often does not know, is that the popular naturalism is itself exceedingly vulnerable. Mention has already been made of the vulnerability of the dogma of determinism. The same is true of Freudianism, of Logical Positivism, of Linguistic Analysis, and of all Materialism. When the Christian moves over to attack, refusing to allow his opponent the advantage of the initiative, he is really following the recorded example of Christ whose intellectual strategy was vividly demonstrated when He said, "I also will ask you a question" (Luke 20:3).

In the effort to provide the ordinary members of the Church with assistance in the fierce struggle in which they are necessarily involved as Christians, a Christian book service is of inestimable value. Good as the spoken word may be, the printed word is better, when it comes to the establishment of a threatened faith, because the printed word can be studied. Its glory lies in its freedom from mere transitoriness. Many readers can remember the time when the ordinary congregation provided no book service at all, the only distributed material being that of the Sunday School *quarterly*. Now this is radically changed, at least on the part of really alert congregations, spurred on by pastors who understand their vocation. Indeed, the presence or absence of a book table is coming to be something of a revelation of the quality of concern in a local Christian fellowship. There are still many who have not caught the idea, but most effective congregations now keep their book tables going every week, with hundreds of volumes distributed in this fashion. The result is sometimes phenomenal, the ordinary members now discussing the sort of books once discussed solely by the professional Christian leaders.

Because there is sometimes confusion on this point, it is necessary to make clear the distinction between a book table and a library. Libraries in church buildings have been in existence for many years and, though they are normally much neglected, they have sometimes performed an important function. A library may reasonably be supplied with the large dictionaries, encyclopedias, and other major works which the members cannot afford to own individually. But, however good the library collection may be, it has only marginal usefulness unless two important conditions are met. First, the physical location of the library must be such that it is readily available and not where people must hunt in order to find it. Second, there must be some person or persons who see the library as an opportunity to engage in a Christian ministry, ordering, arranging, displaying, and informing the potential readers of what is available. Not much of importance occurs in this world without the prodding of deeply devoted persons, and the ministry of books is a vivid example of this fact.

However good the library is, it can never take the place of the book table. The great advantage of actually *selling* the books is that the owners tend to prize them more. Owners will mark books, and will, in many instances, loan them to others. Some committed persons buy several copies of a prized volume at one time in order to have copies on constant loan. If, as a result of this, any of the new readers experience a genuine deepening of convictions, the expenditure is highly justified. Whenever we find a congregation in which the members are building up personal libraries, we can be reasonably sure that this is a strong congregation in other ways.

In some communities there still remains, as a vestige of a false conception of the church building, a resistance to the sale and purchase of books on a table in the foyer or anywhere else on the premises. When this position is expressed it must be attacked directly and unapologetically, because it represents a genuine evil. This evil is the heresy of the idolatry of bricks and mortar, a heresy specifically undermined by the Apostle Paul in Athens when he said, "The God who made the world and everything in it, being Lord of heaven and earth, does not live in shrines made by man" (Acts 17:24). The notion that it is perfectly all right to sell a New Testament in the department store on Monday, but that it is wrong to sell it in the meetinghouse on Sunday, represents a confusion so great that it is truly appalling.

As Christians, we believe in the Real Presence, but it is a severe denial of the divine power to claim that this Presence is limited geographically. If, in a building dedicated to worship, a seeker buys a book on Sunday morning and his life is deepened in consequence, the only important thing to say is that the Gospel has thereby been preached, and this is one of the major tasks of the Church. We are foolish if we do not realize that, human nature being what it is, availability of merchandise makes a crucial difference. It is not at all probable that the seeker who buys the book on Sunday morning would have bothered to hunt it out in a secular store. Of course, he could have done so, but the plain truth is that, normally, he *would* not. We must remember that human lethargy and forgetfulness are remarkable. Part of our task as Christians is to know this and to act accordingly.

As in the case of the library, so, though even more, in the case of the book table, it must have a prominent location, where people practically stumble over it. In retreats, it has been found helpful to place the book table in the dining room where people can examine its offerings both before and after meals. But still more important than location is dedicated supervision on the part of some persons who love books and who are persuasive exponents of their value. In several congregations, otherwise modest members have found a new sense of meaning in their own lives in this ministry of the printed word. They must be readers themselves before they can honorably tell others of the virtue of a book; they must study the catalogues and the book reviews if they are to keep abreast of the times; they must overcome their natural reticence and be bold enough to recommend whatever they prize. A book table never fulfills an important or redemptive function if it stands alone with no supervision and without salesmen. If we have ever supposed that salesmanship is intrinsically evil, this is a judgment which we ought to outgrow. Most of us, in fact, are grateful to some honest salesmen who have made us aware of what we were eventually to prize, though at first we did not do so.

One important aspect of the Christian ministry of books in our time of partial renewal has been the service instituted in the lay academies and retreat houses, which have been established in the last two decades. In practically none of these was there any prevision of the extent of the book service which would be demanded. Now, it has been necessary in each retreat house to expand the book service until it is sometimes the most ambitious single feature of the new enterprise.

Consider, in this connection, the Tri-State Yokefellow House near Defiance, Ohio, from which have been distributed thousands of books in six years of operation. This is a rural area, with many churches, but with no large towns or cities, and with no book service for most of the people, other than that involved in writing to a denominational headquarters. Now all this is changed, because the books go out in a steady stream, especially at the close of each retreat or institute. The sale of *The New English Bible* has been particularly brisk and there has been a wide distribution of the classics of Christian devotion, most of which were utterly unknown to the purchasers until they were confronted in the book store of the attractive old barn which has been transformed, largely by voluntary labor, into an effective Renewal Center for the entire Church, regardless of denomination.

If we take seriously the task of removing the barriers to renewal, we shall endeavor to set up such Christian centers at a variety of different locations, all over the length and the breadth of the land. The local churches cannot do this alone; they need strong points for the gathering of the forces, and this is something which the denominational structure often fails to provide. One of the excellent services which the renewal centers can offer to local congregations is that of providing materials which are hard to assemble. Several of the new houses will send a selection of books which can be had on consignment, thus eliminating all financial risk on the part of the local congregation.[9] Unless some such service is provided we shall not go forward.

---

[9] For the addresses of houses which offer such services, write Yokefellow Associates, 230 College Ave., Richmond, Ind.

The ministry of books requires readers and dedicated sales-men, but, first of all, it requires writers. If the concern for an adequate theology is to be implemented, we must have more writers who learn to think rigorously on the most important questions and who discipline their minds to write in such a way that the rank and file can understand. Far from there being any necessary incompatibility between profundity and clarity, both are required. We have, it is true, a plethora of current books, but we do not have enough good ones. Who, we may reasonably ask, will take the place of the late C. S. Lewis or the late John Baillie? It is practically certain that there are undeveloped literary pow-ers, which are undeveloped chiefly because the possessors of these powers have never thought of themselves as producers. Perhaps the recognition of the minority status of committed Christians may make some of these persons realize that their gifts are needed and that they must, accordingly, be developed. Young Christian writers can help one another to a surprising extent by the sympathetic yet critical reading of one another's manuscripts.

Not all have the ability to write, but all have the ability to loan. One of the finest means of evangelism is that in which a modest person says to his friend, "Here is a book which has reached me. Won't you try it to see if it will answer some of your questions?" The contemporary critic sometimes ridicules the Christian of an earlier generation who passed out tracts, but this is a subject on which we might do well to think again. There is nothing wrong with passing out tracts, provided the tracts are good ones. The contemporary small book can be the modern counterpart of the tract and is usually more effective because it can deal with important questions more fully.[10]

If we could only know it, there are countless new ways of enhancing the spread of this kind of infection. For example, there are a few Christian physicians and dentists who have exper-

[10] In my own experience, I find that a remarkable number of the men and women whose Christian dedication I admire and on whom I depend, were brought to a new sense of the meaning of the Gospel because some person, pastor or layman, loaned a book. Some can tell the day or the hour when a particular sentence opened their eyes.

imented by placing shelves of serious books in their waiting rooms. If any person, with time on his hands, turns to such a shelf when he is tired of the popular magazines, and if, as a result, he gets an idea which is new to him, the entire venture is worth while. One changed life would justify it.

The slowness of modern Christians to see the power of the Lay Academy idea is amazing, because the idea is transparently good. The Christians who have been involved in the Lay Academy development have profited immensely, many becoming ministers in common life, but unfortunately, they still constitute a minority of the Church. The majority still seem satisfied with the more conventional expression of the faith, but their path is the way of death. Eventually the fellowship of the conventional will cease to be a fellowship at all. Each of the lay academies that has been established has been effective, particularly in providing intense weekend educational experiences which the local congregation has not even attempted. Sometimes more changes occur in forty-four hours of such experience than occurs normally in forty-four weeks.

We must now take the next step, already suggested in Chapter 2, and make each local congregation into a Lay Academy, with the pastor as the chief instructor. Because the logic of renewal requires preparation, if the miracle is to occur, we must plan such instruction with care, and this ought to be the major function of each pastor. The book table and the study group become two parts of one whole, and they will always be provided if we really understand that theology is a relevant discipline, not merely for experts, but for everyone who seeks to be Christ's representative in the world.

Though, ideally, each local congregation should see itself as a miniature theological seminary, "rightly handling the word of truth" (II Tim. 2:15), the intellectual and spiritual resources often seem too meager. In this case there can be a very effective middle way, between the local congregation and the established Lay Academy. This middle way is the local Institute of Theology, in which a number of different congregations of various denominations may share a single educational venture. Usually the different pastors teach the classes in a variety of subjects, the instruction proceeding for a limited period of six or eight weeks. Something like this was attempted many years ago, the aim being chiefly that of training Sunday School teachers in a joint effort, but there is no good reason why the work should be thus limited. The idea of a local Institute of Theology is one which may be easily exported from one community to another.[11] The time may come when the local Institute will be as common as the Sunday School has been in the recent past.

A variant on this theme is that in which a pastor, willing to share what he has learned in the theological seminary, will enter into individual learning ventures with particular members or seekers. Many who hope to grow in the faith will surely welcome this kind of personal instruction, which produces as a by-product, a valued relationship between teacher and student. It is a little surprising to learn how many people ask eagerly for reading lists. They mean business, but they do not know where to start. There is undoubtedly a right order in study, and the person who cares about the intellectual aspect of his faith naturally wants to know what this order is.[12]

While we must be practical, if the Church is to be renewed, we must beware of becoming merely institutional. Institutions we clearly need if the good intentions are not to evaporate into nothingness, but we must have more than institutions; we must have genuine communities. In some instances the highly organized institutions are also communities, but this is rare. Everyone who thinks about it knows that there must be the collection and expenditure of funds if modern organizations are to survive, and certainly the first generation of Christians collected funds, but today an inordinate amount goes into salaries and the upkeep of buildings. In some congregations everyone who sings in the choir

[11] For information about a successful Institute at Sunbury, Pa., readers may write to Newman Gaugler, R.F.D., Sunbury, Pa.

[12] A package of nine books, all undoubted classics of Christian devotion, including *The Imitation of Christ* and Law's *A Serious Call,* is now in widespread demand.

is a paid performer. Some of these feel no identification with the fellowship, but do their work faithfully without any sense of belonging. Some secretaries in church offices are not even members!

We have been fortunate in being able to hear some clear voices, warning of the danger of making our church organization into an end rather than a means. One of these is John W. Meister, himself a pastor of an active and highly organized congregation, who is keenly aware of the dangers of the very system in which he is so deeply involved. Dr. Meister maintains that "we have reached a time when conventional American Protestant churches are inordinately concerned with upholding the existence, the authority, and the sanctity of their own organizational structures." Meister goes further to say that, "instead of using organizations to serve people, we use people to serve organizations."[13] One of the chief reasons given by good men who drop out of the professional ministry is that they become unhappy about being primarily promoters. In a similar way, some of the most sensitive of lay seekers resist involvement in church work because they fear, rightly or wrongly, that they are sought chiefly as assets in a business enterprise which must always recruit new contributors if the large promotional budgets are to be maintained.

One reason for the gratifying response to the small group movement in the churches is the obvious contrast between this movement and promotion. When a person is drawn into a little circle, devoted to prayer and to deep sharing of spiritual resources, he is well aware that he is welcomed for his own sake, since the small group has no budget, no officers concerned with the success of their administration, and nothing to promote. A dozen people, sitting in a circle, often listening in silence, and learning to love one another, are sometimes the saving salt even of the Church itself. It is the existence of many such groups within it, which has kept the strong ecclesiastical organization

---

[13] "Requirements for Renewal," *Union Seminary Quarterly Review*, Vol. XVI, No. 3 (March, 1961), p. 4.

which John W. Meister serves from becoming a mere organization.[14] One group of men, with some changes in membership, has met for prayer and for sharing during fourteen unbroken years.

Since all renewal really begins with persons, and there is no renewed Church without renewed individuals, we need to learn how new life can be encouraged. There is no doubt that small groups are a help, though the groups may differ greatly in structure. Fortunately, there is no stereotype to which they must conform. In the Church of the Saviour, in the Nation's Capital, most of these have now become mission groups. But, whatever the structure, the central point is that such groups demonstrate the miracle which occurs whenever there is genuine fellowship. To become members one of another is to unlock secrets of power. It is possible to come to care deeply about a few people and to be lifted by the recognition that the caring is mutual. If the Church is to be genuine, fellowship must be real, and the small group movement is one way in which the growth of true fellowship may be facilitated. The Church, as a "body," is healthy only if it includes healthy cells.

The small fellowship group does not only draw into itself those who are active members; it is also effective in reaching lapsed members. In a number of instances it is found that persons who have dropped out of the public worship of the Church and are loath to return to it when invited to do so, are perfectly willing to join a group in some private house. Once having been reached again by a situation of transparent reality, these persons may later be drawn into the total life of the Church. However valuable public worship is, there are some sensitive people who find it cold and impersonal. Such persons must be reached in other ways, after which the public worship may be more meaningful to them.

There is no possibility of renewal unless we are always living on the spiritual frontier. Of all of the enemies of Christ, none is

[14] The organization mentioned is the First Presbyterian Church, of Fort Wayne, Ind.

more damaging than a tired old religion. We do not know all of the ways in which vitality appears, but we at least know that it will not come by three hymns and a sermon and a conventional benediction. The dying churches are those in which the pulpit is "occupied" and the old record is run off in the presence of persons whose attendance is largely habitual or is produced by a sense of duty. It is obvious that many new developments are possible, but we have not sensed what they are, partly because we have not given the matter the same kind of arduous intellectual attention which research scientists give to the question of the possibility of new products. With no threat whatever to the finality of the Christian revelation, it ought to be possible to discover fresh new ways of expressing it, as we find new ways to make rubber and tape and synthetic fiber.

As we look back at the history of the Church, we are always surprised at the slowness to see the implications of the faith. For instance, it seems strange to us that the first followers of Christ were extremely slow to see that Gentiles could be exactly as close to the Risen Christ as Jews could be, and that the old dietary laws had no relevance whatever. The new opening came to Peter as a distinct wrench and was naturally opposed. Peter saw the idea, but Paul really had to force the door open. Even the casual reader can hardly fail to see the radical difference between the two halves of the Book of Acts, the difference being the result of the emergence of novelty concerning the nature of the field. To us the opening seems obvious, but it was not obvious to the first Christians. In like manner, there are probably equally important developments to which we are still blind, so that our slowness will, in retrospect, seem remarkable to our successors and descendants.

Among the new hints which are coming, though we do not see our way fully in regard to them, may be mentioned "coffee-break evangelism." For better or for worse, the coffee break is now an established part of our culture and, as such, is something to be employed. The gathering of Christian businessmen for a short time each morning, over coffee cups, requires no organization, but only the friendly invitation going from person to person.

One businessman writes of this, in a personal letter, as follows: "When we realize that almost every employed person now has a fifteen-minute coffee break twice a day we suddenly see the opportunity, which churchmen have, to guide conversation during these intervals."

In the Chicago Loop there is a group of committed Christian men who meet for luncheon once a week, not in imitation of the standard luncheon club with its grim necessity of a program each week, but to share what they are reading and thinking. Sometimes all of the men are reading simultaneously the same book. Thus it is possible to meet a longfelt need in secular life with the kind of novelty that ought to be part of Christian experience.

If we understand that religion is not something separate from common life, but a particular way of dealing with daily experience, there are many occasions to be interpreted and glorified by the alert Church. A good example, in recent years, was provided when, on the death of T. S. Eliot, a special service of thanksgiving for Eliot's life and witness was held at Harvard and was located, appropriately, in Memorial Church. Various professors read aloud from Eliot's poetry, the Church providing a uniting center for the many aspects of the brilliant man's life. The gatherings in Washington, sponsored by the National Presbyterian Church, and held immediately prior to each Congress, is an example of how the Church, when it is open to freshness, may give spiritual meaning to secular occasions.

At the heart of the logic of all renewal is the recognition that there is no changed Church without changed lives among the members. There are no external tricks which are really effective. The well-known classic statement of this important truth is in the words of William Penn when he wrote, in reference to the first explosive generation of Quakers, "They became changed men themselves before they went out to change others." A contemporary expression of the same basic theme is that of Billy Graham, "Christ can save the world only as He is living in the hearts of men and women."[15] We seek a new order in the world, but the order will not be established by legislation or by social

15 *World Aflame, op. cit.,* p. 178.

engineering, important as these may be. We need only to give attention to the crass politicking and corruption of the Anti-Poverty Program and the Job Corps to overcome any naïve faith we may have about man's ability to save the world by means of a system. The real enemy is always the sin of self-centeredness in the human heart, and this can find a way of entering into any system, including ecclesiastical ones, which the human mind can contrive. This is why there is not and cannot be any substitute for the experience of full inner commitment to Christ. All persons, whether they are nuclear scientists or space travelers or shoe salesmen or housewives, have the same essential dangers, whatever their level of education.

Commitment is a necessary beginning, but it is far from being the end. Beyond commitment there is a vast amount of necessary toil, which cannot be accomplished without the glad acceptance of personal discipline. The renewed Church must be the disciplined fellowship of disciplined persons. The Christian who rejects inner controls, supposing that free self-expression is the essence of the Gospel, will never contribute to the renewal of the Church. Once this was said by a few, but now, thankfully, it is being said by thousands. In addition to the familiar disciplines of regular prayer, Bible reading and proportionate giving, some are now experimenting with the practice of fasting. We can remember when this practice was considered laughable, but the mood is beginning to change, particularly when thoughtful people consider how important fasting was in Biblical times. A retreat has been held recently in which, at noon, the retreatants gathered at tables, but wholly without the confusion of food. All appreciated the change, partly because they recognized that they tended to eat too much.

One important fresh development, which began in the John Wesley Methodist Church of Tallahassee, Florida, and which has subsequently spread to other cities, particularly to Louisville, Kentucky, is that in which the hard disciplines are accepted, in the beginning, for only one experimental month. The psychological advantage of this is apparent, because there are many sincere

persons who hesitate to accept a discipline for all the rest of
the time, yet will gladly try it for thirty days. It was found, in the
Louisville experience, that a number of Christians who hesitated
to tithe all year, were perfectly glad to give one tenth of their
total income during the month of August. The happy outcome is
that a considerable proportion of the experimenters have volun-
tarily decided to continue a practice which meant much more
than they expected it to mean. They found that they were glad
to be part of a movement in which discipleship really meant
something, and a surprising proportion of these have now gone
on from mere discipleship to apostleship.

It is important to make clear that a disciplined fellowship
never emerges if the discipline is presented as a vague and general idea; it must be made explicit. For example, many in the
Church really want to engage in daily Bible reading, but they
simply do not know how to do so. It has been discovered that
much more is accomplished, in this regard, if there is a definite
plan. Ideally the plan includes the reading of an entire Biblical
book in successive days, limiting the daily reading to eleven or
twelve verses. The Gospel of Mark can be read in this way in
sixty days. If the discipline is practiced faithfully for two months,
and if the passages read are marked and dated each day, so that
the record is a check on self-delusion, the probability of going on
with the practice in succeeding months is surprisingly great.

Because the Christian Movement is still young and therefore
flexible, fresh openings are possible on every side. Consequently
the Church of the future may be very different from the Church
known in the past or even today. The golden text of Christian
novelty is "It does not yet appear what we shall be" (I John
3:2). In a mechanical order the future is predetermined by the
past, but the Christian is convinced that the ultimate basis of
order is more than mechanical. Because God is, the order is
purposive, and purpose leads to newness.

The logic of renewal, when we understand even a little of it,
makes us see that our principle is the principle of development.
There is no good reason why Christian institutions should not

change with the years. There is no fixed creed about the social order or the achievement of peace or the character of the Christian ministry. Development is an alternative principle both to the fixity of the past and to contempt for the past. The way of growth is to follow the tested insights with such faithfulness that we are led to see new applications of them.

If Marx was right, nothing that is really new occurs, but the Christian Church is not Marxist. This is the point of a sentence from the pen of one of the chief architects of Church Renewal, Stephen Neill. "Now history," he writes, "is always the scene of the unpredictable and the unexpected."[16] The best theology makes us know that the world is the laboratory for God's purposes and that, because men and women, in spite of all of their sins, are made in God's image, they can share in the embodiment of these purposes. They are part of history and history is the scene of the emergence of the new.

---

[16] *Christian Faith and Other Faiths, op. cit.,* p. 8.

CHAPTER 4

The Base and the Field

Only if nothing is profane can anything be sacred.
                                        —William Temple

The hardest problem of Christianity is the problem of the Church. We cannot live without it, and we cannot live with it. In practice the local congregation is nearly always disappointing and there are many separate reasons for our disappointment. The annual conferences of the denominations usually meet in large halls, but such space is seldom needed, because, at most sessions, there are so many empty seats. One reason for the empty seats is the nearly uniform dullness of the procedures. Sometimes the church deliberations bear a remarkable similarity to those of a political gathering, for which the real decisions are made behind the scenes. Sometimes the self-seeking is truly shocking, the leaders seeming to be more concerned for power than for principles. That this is no new phenomenon is easily seen by a careful study of Paul's Letters, especially the Letters to the Corinthians. The failure of the Church has been going on from the earliest days of its history.

If this were the whole story we might end in despair, but we are well aware that it is not the whole story. However bad the Church may be in practice it is the necessary vehicle for Christ's penetration of the world. Even though it is normally much adulterated, the Church is now, as always, the saving salt. The intelligent plan, then, is never to abandon the Church, but, instead, to find some way of restoring the salt. All three of the Synoptic Gospels ask the practical question about the saving salt, which states vividly the sharpness of the option open to us. The question is phrased by Christ in such a way as to indicate that there is no other alternative, in addition to that of the presence of the salt on the one hand, and complete cultural disaster on the other. If the salt is lost, all is lost! This is made clear by asking what other element is a candidate for the redemptive task. "If the salt has lost its saltness, how will you season it?" (Mark 9:50). The Church can, Jesus indicates, become so adulterated in its own character that it is no longer an antidote to decay and is then absolutely worthless, but the encouraging fact is that, in most areas, such total failure has not yet occurred.

Of the many contributions made to our generation by William Temple none is more profound than that of his accent on the necessity of the Church. "Christ," he reminded us, "wrote no book; He left in the world as His witness a 'body' of men and women on whom His spirit came."[1] It is a great insight to realize that the primary witness to Christ is a living society. Whenever we meditate upon the inadequacy of the individual members of this society, including ourselves, we are always shocked and humbled by the oddity of the arrangement. We are wholly accustomed to the existence of various forms of organizations and institutions, but the Church defies classification as one of them.

Most of the uniqueness of the Church is involved in its peculiar relationship to the world. Always, since the beginning, there has been the glaring paradox that the Church exists *for the sake of* the world, yet is *different from* the world. The salt exists for the sake of the meat, but is never identical *with* that which it penetrates. The same relationship is equally obvious when we employ the parallel metaphors of light and leaven. In spite of its failures, it is always the case that, in the life of the Church, the standard of behavior is one which the world is not willing to

---

[1] *Readings in St. John's Gospel* (London: Macmillan & Co., Ltd., 1955), p. xvi.

adopt. The worldly rulers seek for prestige, their search for self-advancement being sweetened by efforts to establish reputations as benefactors, "but not so with you" (Luke 22:26).

In view of the evidence presented, in Chapter 1, for the proposition that Christians are and have always been a minority people, the Christian word "parish" becomes far more meaningful. The word "parish" comes from a Greek word meaning "a body of aliens in the midst of any community." The New Testament uses this term, with some variations in the application, in Acts 7:6, 29, Ephesians 2:19, and I Peter 2:11. The Petrine use is particularly clear, "I beseech you as aliens or exiles." The consequence was that the earliest Christians used similar language to indicate the peculiar status of their separated fellowships. A parish, then, was inevitably an *enclave*. Often it was wholly surrounded by the contemptuous and the antagonistic. The popular view is that this situation is now wholly obsolete, but there is strong evidence that the popular view, on this issue, is incorrect. There is deep wisdom in the Christian determination to unite in parishes, since this is the only way in which the saltness can be retained.

An insistent question which Christians keep asking themselves, and one another, concerns the location of the Church. Where, we ask, is the Church? By trying to answer this question truthfully we may find that we are also answering, at the same time, several other insistent questions. But it is probable that the majority of people think that the question is a slightly ridiculous one because, they believe, the answer is so obvious. Ask the average man on the street where the Westminster Presbyterian Church is and he will answer that it is across from the Greyhound Bus Station. What he means is that this is the physical location of the building which belongs to, and is sometimes used by members of a particular congregation. It is not hard to see why, in the popular mentality, this identification is almost universally made. If one sends a letter to the congregation it will be delivered to the above-designated address. Furthermore, since the sign in front of the building says "Westminster Presbyterian Church," the people naturally think that the physical structure is, itself, the Church. Therefore, to ask its location seems to be a foolish question.

It helps us to be reminded that, so far as the earliest Christians were concerned, the question of the location of the Church, if it had been asked, could not have received the facile answer now ordinarily given. Though it is a bit shocking to modern men, accustomed as they are to ecclesiastical real estate, the truth is that the Christians of the first three centuries appear not to have owned anything. The resident of Corinth, in A.D. 55, could have identified, with no trouble at all, the location of the Temple of Apollo, but the question of the location of the Church of Christ would have stumped him. He could not have pointed to the church building at Fifteenth and Main, because there was no such structure in existence.

The present tendency to identify the Church and the building is a more profound error than it at first appears to be. The error is the error of all segregation. If the Christian witness is relegated to a building, with four walls, the harm comes, not in what occurs within these particular walls, but in the consequent easing of the conscience about what goes on elsewhere. If the Christian emphasis of a college is identified with one particular week of the academic year, or limited to that period, the evil consists, not in the events of that week, but in what is omitted from the other fifty-one weeks. If the Church is identified too closely with a particular spot, the problem arises in all the other spots. Thus, religious segregation need not be merely racial, but can be both temporal and spatial.

We begin to see how much more important the question of the location of the Church is than it seems to be, when we see how the question affects even the great idea of the lay ministry, which has been discussed in previous chapters. The lay ministry is often short-circuited by being tied too closely to the institutional structure, symbolized by the building. It is not really very difficult to recruit laymen to do more *inside* the Church, but the sad result is that, in that case, they tend to become clericalized laymen. "By concentrating their energies inside the Church," says Colin Williams, "the vision of their lay ministries in the world has been lost."[2]

The recognition that concentration of the work of members *within the Church* is a serious mistake is one of the real gains in understanding in our generation. One result is that a good many now have an answer to the question of the location of the Church which is almost as facile as is the popular or conventional answer of the recent past. Indeed, we seem to be on the way to the establishment of a new convention. The fashionable contemporary answer, provided now by those who have done some reading of current discussions of Church Renewal, is the simple one that the location of the Church is in the world. The real undertaking, they say, does not go on within the Church, imperfect and squabbling as it is, but in offices and factories and homes and schools. The manning of the trenches begins, not on Sunday morning, but on Monday.

The mistake of this answer, as is the case with most simple answers, lies not in what it affirms, but in what it omits. The tendency of the new convert to this now modish way of thinking is to affirm that what takes place in the meetinghouse at Fifteenth and Main is utterly unimportant or irrelevant. As the horrible new jargon puts it, the need is to be where the action is, and the action, it is confidently said, is not in the church building. Therefore, it seems to follow, we must put our entire emphasis upon the coffee house and the United Nations and the Peace Corps and the hours spent in the factory. It is not a caricature to say that some now suppose that full acceptance of what is popularly known as "worldly Christianity" involves the abandonment of the Church as a separate entity, and that many alleged Christians have only contempt for the parish Church.

The current emphasis on the worldliness of Christianity, while it involves an element of strength, is also full of dangers. Some Christian leaders try to prove how worldly they are by an exhibi-

[2] *Where in the World?* (New York: World Council of Churches, 1963), p. 81.

tion of profanity. Though we may appreciate their rejection of mere pietism, it is easy to see that these rebels are putting on a sophomoric pose that is not likely to impress even those whom they most desire to reach. The new secularism has also involved a sentimental glorification of the "city" or "metropolis," as though it were a place of innate loveliness. This is easy to understand, because the people who go to this extreme are clearly reacting against the domination of the Christian scene by the rural ideal. They want their readers to see that there is sin in the country, to which the relevant answer is, "Yes, certainly, but there is also sin in the city, with its political bosses and corruption on every side." Error, as Aristotle taught the world, may be multiple. The fact that the country can be vicious does not mean that the metropolis is to be identified with the Kingdom of Christ. The Church in the Wildwood is surrounded by sin, but so is the Church in Times Square.

One of the striking revelations of the new theology is that the merely worldly Christianity may be as much a failure as is the unworldly Christianity in which many contemporary Christians were nurtured. For example, just having a coffee house doesn't do the trick! Several of the coffee houses, supposedly modeled on the Potter's House, on Columbia Road, in Washington, have not survived. What their organizers have failed to notice is that the Washington coffee house, supported as it is by the Church of the Saviour, is only one part of a necessary polarity. What the casual visitor sees, when he sits at a table at the Potter's House, is one thing, but a necessary condition of the effectiveness is the separated and self-conscious life of the Church, of which the visitor is probably ignorant.

The science of dialogue with the world seems not to be effective unless it arises as a result of a continuing fellowship of those who love one another and who maintain a conscious existence separate from the world. Beyond the public witness lies the life of devotion, of prayer groups, and of prayer for one another over long periods. The relevant fact is that several of the coffee houses, which have closed, have lacked this other pole. They became *mere* coffee houses and that, naturally, is the end of the chapter. There is grave doubt whether there can be effective witness in the world unless there is, at some point, a deep and unapologetic piety. Those who reject piety, because of their youthful revolt against its aberrations, are likely to kill the thing which they love. The love of the brethren is likely to be more genuine if there is, at the same time, an unabashed expression of the Love of Christ.

The point just made, if true, is a very important one. It means that the only hope for the renewal of the Church lies in the recognition of its essential polarity. The Church must exist *in* the world, but, paradoxically, it must exist, at the same time, *apart from* the world. What occurs, when the little fellowship gathers, need not be irrelevant and it is never irrelevant if it strengthens men and women for their inevitable encounter with worldly principalities and powers. The *witness*, it is important to realize, must be made in the metropolis, but the *preparation* for the witness is best carried on in the society of those who know that, as "parishioners," they are sojourners or aliens in the metropolis and elsewhere.

We are making a great step forward when we realize that there is no inevitable contradiction between the idea of the scattered Church and the idea of the gathered Church. We gather in order to scatter! The Church is a particular fellowship of men and women involved in common life, sharing the life of Christ, who assemble with one another for the purpose of *sending*. Christians are perpetually being "sent out" (Mark 6:7), but they cannot be sent out unless they have already been *drawn in*. The Christian operation, which never ends, is that according to which Disciples are continually being turned into Apostles, but members must be Disciples first. What is the use of being sent out if men have nothing to give when they arrive? How can dialogue with the world be worth anything if the saints have nothing to say?

One conclusion of such an analysis is that the continued existence of the local Church is necessary for the total Christian enterprise. If it is necessary, we are justified in devoting a great deal of thought, time, and energy into the task of making it what it ought to be. Because service without piety is only one sad example of the inevitable failure of a cut-flower civilization, it is important for us to give our thoughtful attention to the nurture of the little fellowships which keep the roots alive.

Though I am as conscious as are most people of the inadequacies of the local Church, and though I am sure that the Church is not the building, I can never pass a little building devoted to Christ's cause without a sense of reverence and the utterance of a short prayer of thanksgiving. I know, by sad experience, how dull the Adult Bible Class probably is, and I could repeat many of the stereotyped testimonies of the Prayer Meeting; I know, furthermore, how great the likelihood is that the pastor is an unimaginative man; but I know some other things as well. I know that it was in such ugly buildings that many of our Christian leaders first learned to sing God's praise and to hear the marvelous cadences of the Psalms. Furthermore, I can never forget that, apart from the poor little fellowships in such poor little buildings, there isn't a chance in the world that I would be enlisted today in the cause of Christ. In my youth I was impressed by seeing devout Roman Catholics tip their hats, as the street cars passed the doors of their church buildings. I am tempted to do the same whenever I pass a place in which the love of Christ has been consciously nourished and where I know simple men have prayed. Because I can never see such a place without a sense of wonder, aware as I am of the sacrifice on the part of so many, which has made the place possible, I can never join in the fashionable depreciation of "place." The value of the place is not in itself, for that would entail idolatry, but rather in the recognition that there is no available power unless it emanates from a center. It was necessary, Christ said, for the Apostles to gather at Jerusalem before they could be effective witnesses in the world.

The necessity of recognizing both sides of the polarity was expressed vividly by Richard Niebuhr as he struggled to avoid the heresy of simplification in either direction. "The movement

)f withdrawal and renunciation," he said, "is a necessary element in every Christian life, even though it be followed by an equally necessary movement of responsible engagement in cultural tasks."[3]

The paradox of the gathered and scattered Church is made more understandable by reference to the experience of the Iona Community, both ancient and modern. A brilliant interpretation of the basic Iona idea is that of *We Shall Rebuild* by George MacLeod. The contemporary Iona Fellowship which is largely the result of the creative imagination of Dr. MacLeod, is inspired by Columba's pattern of evangelism. This pattern involved both a *base* and a *field*. The base was the little Island of Iona, which has, in recent centuries, inspired so many visitors, including Doctor Samuel Johnson.

When mainland Scotland was an undeveloped and unevangelized country, how was the bold and resourceful Columba to begin? He saw his work as divided between gathering and scattering. His workers gathered on the isolated island, apart from the "world," until they were ready, and then they scattered over the mainland. There they taught the people to read, to appreciate the Bible, to work iron, to bake bread, and much else. Then, when the evangelists were very tired, they returned to Iona to recuperate, to gather their forces, and to get ready to scatter again. MacLeod's dream in our generation is that of the duplication of this pattern.

One of the important insights which has come to several, in the contemporary struggle for Church Renewal, is that the "base and field" pattern can be applied, without distortion, to the regular work of the ordinary congregation, whatever the location and whatever the denomination. The field, in which the members, who are normally termed laymen, are to work and witness is the ordinary world of business, of scholarship, of professional competence, and of domesticity. Each Monday morning the evangelists sail for the mainland! The base, by contrast, is the gathered congregation, where the worldly evangelists come together to

[3] *Christ and Culture, op. cit.,* p. 68.

strengthen one another in prayer, in testimony, in the study of the Gospel, and in learning from one another the art of witness. Because the fight on the front line is often fierce, the troops need a time behind the lines in which to gather their strength. Experience shows that this is best done, so far as Christians are concerned, in an atmosphere of mutual trust. The renewal of the workers at the base is not likely to occur unless there is a genuine *koinonia*.

Careful consideration of the Iona model makes us realize that every Christian must be prepared to live a "double life." In the world it is important that he be as wise as a serpent; at the base it is important that he be as harmless as a dove. The Church as a base must be as unlike the world as possible, in that it must be a place in which the struggle for power and prestige is rejected or transcended. There is no possibility of building up the Church unless, at each local base, we have a restoration of true fellowship. We must never forget that, so far as the New Testament is concerned, *koinonia* is not something added, but something which belongs to the very nature of the Church. A base is not a true Christian base unless it is a center of affection, in which the members accept the principle of unlimited liability for one another. Every sensible person knows that unlimited liability is impossible in the business world, but the definition of the Christian fellowship is that in which it *is* possible.

In the light of the Iona pattern, we are now in a position to answer the question of what the location of the Church is. It is located in two places, a place of retirement and a place of exposure. Heresy, then, comes in either of two ways. It is a heresy to limit the Church to the base, for then the central purpose of penetration of the world is denied. This heresy exists in varying degrees, the extreme form being that of the Amish Brethren whose base is very strong, but whose conception of the field is nil. It is likewise a heresy, and one which requires careful elaboration now, to limit the Church to the world. The tendency to have worldly Christianity, and nothing but worldly Christianity, would mean the eventual death of the Church, because the central root would be severed. Shocking as it is to say so, it is important to remember that churches can die. There is the sad record of some which *have* died, the most striking example being the Church of North Africa, which once included such powerful minds as those of Tertullian, of Cyprian, and of the great Augustine of Hippo. According to Harnack, the strongest of all Christian influences emanated for a while from Africa, and then the African Church died. Death comes when the essential balance is lost, and the balance we most need to encourage now is that which is represented by polarity.

In each generation we tend to overstate some position which, though a valid one, becomes heretical when overstressed or stressed in isolation. Thus, we can have real admiration for many of the efforts of the pietist movement, which certainly produced some beautiful lives, but it is easy to see that the whole temptation was to minimize the work in the field, while emphasizing the nurture at the base. In the late nineteenth century Hannah Whitall Smith was marvelously effective in stressing the purity of the inner Christian life, with the result that *The Christian's Secret of a Happy Life* has sold at least two million copies in the last ninety years, but Mrs. Smith had almost nothing to say about the social gospel.

Today, our danger is one which is the opposite of that inherent in Mrs. Smith's valuable contribution. Writers, of the past decade, have so stressed the work of the Christian in the everyday life of the metropolis that some are almost ashamed to give any time to the little congregation in the neighborhood. We are reminded of the famous dictum of John Stuart Mill that men are generally right in what they affirm and wrong in what they deny. It is important to affirm that "the field is the world," but it is equally important not to deny that "the good seed means the sons of the kingdom" (Matt. 13:38). This seed is not preserved except in a conscious loving fellowship.

Once we are convinced of the necessity of the fellowship which is, in one sense, unworldly, we are ready to direct our best thought to the new forms which membership in such a fellowship should take. In the past few centuries it has been agreed, without argument and even without serious examination, that the primary basis of membership ought to be *residential*. Thus, the parish, i.e., the company of sojourners, constitutes an enclave which is geographical. The parish has come to mean, by definition, a particular geographical unit of people, who gather in a building near the place where most of them live. What we need to face now, with all of the courage which we can muster, is the fact that, today, such a residential unit is increasingly fictitious. The Community Church idea, once a valid one, is such no longer, and it has been rendered invalid by ease of mobility. If people step into automobiles to go a distance of two miles, there is no significant reason for not going six. Consequently, in the experience of the normal congregation, people come from a wide scattering of areas. The Church, west of the river, may count half of its members among those who live east of the river.

Sometimes we deplore the fact that members live at a considerable distance from the building in which they gather, but this is a waste of tears, because the situation is not likely to change by anything which we can do. The automobile, along with other features of our technology, has made man's place of residence essentially insignificant. This point is sometimes made vividly by saying that people do not live where they live! What is meant is that they do not live solely or even primarily where they reside. They live in buses; they live in factories; they live in public dining rooms; they live in offices; they live in clubs. Often a man, whose address is in the suburbs, arrives home after dark and leaves, in the winter, before daylight. There is a good chance that he is not personally acquainted with any of the other men on his street, though he may share wisdom with a few about the cultivation of roses, as the men work in their flower gardens on Saturday afternoons and Sundays. There is no more reason why he should develop Christian fellowship with his horticultural acquaintances than with a host of others.

What we must understand is that rejection of residential membership is not a total rejection of the membership idea. Already people go miles to help produce a Christian base, both for themselves and for others, who live miles in the opposite direction. The point is that this mobility, far from being absurd, makes good sense. Perhaps the best bases ought to be arranged in the light of vocation. One of the finest fellowships we have known has been made up principally of a group of committed physicians, and why not? These men prize their work far more highly than they prize their suburban street addresses.

It is conceivable that there should be great variety in the bases that are established. For example, there is much to be said for a deep fellowship on the part of people who are so devoted to evangelism, particularly on Sundays, that they could not reasonably be expected to maintain a separate public gathering on Sunday morning. But this need not be a barrier, provided we are emancipated from the stereotype. It is not hard to imagine a group which finds its real *koinonia* on one evening in the week, as is done regularly by Alcoholics Anonymous, with the expectation that the members serve in dozens of different places on Sundays. Ordinarily, the rhythm of the Church is such that there should be the establishment of the base on Sunday and the scattering during the week, but, since there is nothing sacred about particular days, there is no good reason why, in particular instances, this pattern should not be reversed.

Both Methodists and Presbyterians have learned the wisdom of not expecting their pastors to be members of local congregations. Instead, they belong to Conferences and Presbyteries. As the lay ministry grows, there ought to be a similar arrangement for the nonclerical ministers, especially for those whose travel responsibilities are such that they can seldom gather regularly at any one place on Sundays. When we think of George Fox in the seventeenth century we realize that it would have been a tragic mistake to limit him to one congregation. Fox has many counterparts in the modern Christian scene, including those who work for Church Boards and who teach in colleges. But such people are to be reminded that, if they do not have the steady Sunday morning fellowship, they still need some other to take its place.

The deepest clue to the miracle of recovery which occurred at Coventry in 1962 and 1963 and which we shall describe in Chapter 5, was the discovery, on the part of the clergymen involved, that they needed a steady fellowship and this they found in the weekly gathering of pastors. This soon became the hub, of which the parish work was the wheel.[4]

We have traveled far in our understanding of what the Church ought to be when we realize that, for the Christian, membership involves two loyalties. The Churchman must be loyal to the world because the Church exists for the world's sake, but he must also be loyal to the fellowship which is the center of his new life in Christ. Karl Barth has expressed this double responsibility by saying, "Faithfulness of the Church to the world is after all possible only as the reverse side of an entirely different loyalty."[5] We may put it another way by saying that the Christian fellowship, in order to be true to its vocation, must always be both Christ-centered and service-minded. The unfortunate fact is that great sections of the Church are satisfied to be one or the other of these, apart from the needed supplement. Though, in the following sentences, Canby Jones was speaking only of contemporary Quakers, his words apply, unfortunately, to members of many other denominations.

Oh, how Friends need to come together! How they need one another! How much the Christ-centered Quakers need to *do* and to serve, to act as Jesus the servant did and to follow in his steps. On the other hand, how much the "humanist" or "service-minded" Friends need to see humanitarian concern fulfilled and climaxed and all humanity reconciled to God and to one another through God's Servant-Messiah from whose love all selfless service springs.[6]

---

[4] See Stephen Verney, *Fire in Coventry* (Westwood, N. J.: Fleming H. Revell Company, 1964).

[5] *God in Action*, translated by E. G. Homrighausen and Karl J. Ernst (Manhasset: Round Table Press, 1963), p. 28.

[6] Jones, "The Concept of Christ as Servant as Motivation to Quaker Service," *Quaker Religious Thought*, Vol. V, No. 2 (Autumn, 1963), p. 39.

Dr. Jones, in the article just quoted, describes our sad situation vividly by pointing out the degree to which we are "divided between those who support service and not missions, and those who support missions and not service."[7] This division is the one to which we should pay close attention now, because it is the division which really hurts the contemporary Church. It has far more contemporary relevance than does the old division between evangelicals and liberals, a division which is increasingly meaningless as our real predicament becomes clear to us. The most tragic divisions are those between two aspects of a whole in which both are needed because each needs the other. The current form of such division is that which makes Christians satisfied to stress the base alone or the field alone.

How shall the Church be loyal to the world which is its field? We are better able to answer this question when it becomes clear to us what the world is. It is the entire secular culture, made up of governments, publishing houses, libraries, schools, labor unions, and innumerable homes with their television sets and cars and flower gardens. Anything that is part of the human experiment is the field of operation. In short, evangelism, to be genuine, must be total. The task of the Church, as the redemptive unit, is staggering, precisely because it includes "all the world" (Mark 16:15). Though, on the face of the matter, this is an impossible task, the Church has long known the practical relevance of such an impossible requirement. It is so truly humbling that the member of the Church, on whom an impossible burden is laid, is moved to pray, with John Wilhelm Rowntree, "Then, O Christ, convince us by Thy Spirit, thrill us with Thy Divine passion, drown our selfishness in Thy invading love, lay on us the burden of the world's suffering, drive us forth with the Apostolic fervour of the early Church!"

It is part of the glory of the Church that the task of penetrating the whole world is, when fully understood, a means of encouragement rather than of despair. The magnitude and seeming impossibility of the undertaking tends to discourage us, but we

[7] *Ibid.*, p. 40.

are encouraged when we realize that we do not work merely in our own power. The Christian who understands his calling is humble for two reasons: first, the demand exceeds his powers, and, second, the essential calling is that of a servant. This is the fundamental reason why all committed Christians must see themselves as ministers. It is good to remind ourselves, over and over, that servant and minister are fundamentally the same word. The ultimate sacrament is that of the washing of the feet of those who are less privileged than ourselves.

Once we have the clear idea that the relation of the base to the field is essentially one of servanthood, we need to rethink constantly what service means. We are likely to fall into the mistake of supposing that the only service is "organized" service. This is the mistake of the young people who, in the summer, resist taking ordinary jobs on ordinary farms or in factories because, they say, they want to "serve." Their meaning is that they want to enlist in work camps which will operate in Africa or in some American slum. We ought, of course, to support these organized efforts, but we ought, at the same time, to resist the idea that these are the sole or even the chief forms which service in the world can take. In referring to the lamentable division between that part of the Church which is "Christ-centered" and that which is "service-minded," Dr. Arthur Roberts makes a telling point about the danger of limiting the concept of service to that which is arranged by a committee.

Is the man who repairs automobiles "serving" the Kingdom only if he is sent as a missionary or joins the Peace Corps? Is the poor Quaker youth who works summers picking beans among the transients denied service in favor of the more prosperous youth who goes to Mexico to teach village children how to play softball? Is service done only when organized by a committee? Are we not to serve in the normal vocations of life?[8]

[8] *Ibid.*, p. 44.

We can be grateful to Arthur Roberts for warning against the danger of fraudulence in our service theme. Though he makes the point by asking questions, it is clear that he believes that the chief form of service for most Christians must be found in the normal vocations of life. And in this he is brilliantly right. There is a serious danger that young people will rush into service projects with very little to give. The world needs people who are competent engineers and doctors and industrialists and secretaries. These tasks are more demanding and harder to learn than is a game of softball. All important service comes at a high personal price. It is not easy to learn languages, or to learn to write with clarity, or to learn to speak honestly and persuasively, or to manage a computer.

In cultivating his field, then, the Christian must at least be equal to others in competence, while his commitment adds something which the world sorely needs. For example, we need a great many men and women who combine the commitment of the unapologetic Christian with the competence of the first-rate scientist. There is a serious linguistic loss in the fact that the term "Christian Scientist" has been identified, in our culture, with a particular denomination. We need a great many more Christian scientists because science is one of the truly formative elements in the total life of modern man, as it never has been before. Until the beginning of our century, technology was relatively independent of science, many of the inventors of machines not being scientists at all, but working only empirically. Now all of this is radically changed. Since the emergence of what is sometimes called the Second Industrial Revolution, very few advances have come to pass as the result of work by scientific amateurs. No one now supposes that it is possible to do first-rate work in the field of metals without a disciplined understanding of how X-ray diffraction will show the arrangement of the atoms. In short, no one can any more do adequate work in technology if he deals only with items that are directly observable. This truth has been vividly expressed by Professor C. A. Coulson, Rouse Ball Professor of

Mathematics at Oxford University, when he says, "For technology now depends on science."[9]

Professor Coulson's own work is a brilliant example of what is meant when, in contemporary church life, we talk about moving from the base to the field, and back again. On one side of his life, Coulson is a distinguished scientist, a Fellow of the Royal Society, especially skilled in the mathematical laws of physics. On the other side of his life, his clear motivation is the love of Christ, about which he is refreshingly unapologetic and forthright. When we know this, we are not surprised to learn that he is a lay minister in the Methodist Church. When he was assigned the enviable task of giving the Beckly Lectures, he had a magnificent chance to deal with the supposedly outworn topic of science and religion in really fresh ways. The topic has not often been handled by men whose scientific competence and Christian conviction are equally matched. Coulson sees, on the one hand, "the tremendous involvement of science and technology in the pattern of our lives," and, on the other hand, that, apart from the insights which Christians possess, "wrong decisions are certain to be made."[10]

Unless the witness of Christ's Church somehow relates to the Second Industrial Revolution, it is bound to seem merely antique, for this revolution is going to cover the earth. What men do in Indiana they can do in Kenya. If we did not know it already, many of us were convinced, by reading Sir Charles Snow's book *The Two Cultures and the Scientific Revolution*, of how easily and quickly technology can be learned. But will it be learned in a way really helpful to men and women? In what spirit should the new technology come to the world? *This is a question which technology does not answer.* Many of us will undoubtedly live to see steel factories, pharmaceutical houses, and uranium-powered electric generators all over our little earth,

---

[9] *Science, Technology and the Christian* (Nashville: Abingdon Press, 1960), p. 19.
[10] *Ibid.*, p. 7.

but one would need to be exceedingly naïve to suppose that such developments will be necessarily beneficent. Whether these will be a boon or a burden depends neither on the amount of money available nor on the technical know-how, both of which can easily be prostituted to unworthy ends. Professor Coulson gives part of his own answer when he writes:

It will depend upon whether the personal relationships involved are recognized and dealt with—the sacrifice among the wealthy nations, the acceptance of charity among the poorer ones, the mutual trust which alone makes cooperation fruitful. All these are possible only if we have a worthy view of man. Technology, without this, may do infinite harm. But with it, it may become a tool in the shaping of the Kingdom of Heaven on earth.[11]

The absolutely necessary contribution from the base to the field is the conviction that every man is a creature made in the image of the Living God, who is like Christ. It is the responsibility of the Church, if it is to take seriously the humbling vocation of being leaven in the lump, to establish and to clarify a pattern of thought, in terms of which decisions may be made and actions judged. When scientists are honest, as most of them are, they are well aware of the fact that their competence in science does not give them a clue to the problem of how their science should be used in the service of man. The sensitive visitor to the mesas of Los Alamos is almost sure to meditate on the experience of that gifted man, Klaus Fuchs. Though his work in the laboratories was outstanding, his decision concerning the use of what he knew was disastrous. What if, in addition to his scientific competence, the younger Fuchs had shared something of the Christian conviction of his father, Emil Fuchs? Much of the subsequent history of our earth might then have been different. Would there, for example, be a wall in Berlin?

It is high time for Christians to understand that what they

[11] *Ibid.*, p. 103.

have to contribute to the culture of the world is not some superficial polish, but an ingredient which may make all the difference between glory and disaster. "The role of the Christian community as such," says Coulson, "is not to do the science, or devise the technology, or form some new political party; it is to see the need of all these, to welcome them as gifts of God; and then to think creatively, bringing all these aspects of human toil together."[12]

We are not likely to bring these aspects of toil together unless there is a more conscious dedication of Christians to a new upsurge of penetration. The basic Christian insights will not be brought to bear on the technological revolution except through persons who are themselves committed to these insights. Nothing will occur in abstraction. There is a tremendous need for trained engineers, especially in India and in Africa, but what a difference it would make if a considerable share of the membership of a volunteer engineer corps were made up of Christians who would carry their Christian motivation into their work! The philosopher-president of India has said, on a visit to America, that the great failure of Indian higher education is its failure to train engineers. From ten to twenty thousand could be used at once. Without them there will be recurring famines as long as we can foresee the future at all.

What a powerful idea it is to consider the recruitment of a Corps of Christian Engineers, each member of the Corps having the double qualification of engineering competence and warmhearted acceptance of Christian conviction about God and man! There must be thousands who would be able to take early retirement and consequently to engage in an entirely new chapter at less pay, all because they are enlisted in Christ's service. Their purpose would not be to enhance the reputation of any particular denomination or board, but to bring to bear on the world's need the combination of elements which are too often separated. The tough-minded conclusion to which we are forced to give assent is that technology, like patriotism, is not enough. It requires something to be added. It needs the motivation which

[12] *Ibid.*, p. 109.

would hardly be known in the world had the Gospel not appeared.

Science-grounded technology is not the only example of how the Christian fellowship can and should penetrate the world revealed by science. Another illustration is provided by the work of Loren Eiseley, professor of anthropology and the history of Science at the University of Pennsylvania. When Professor Eiseley produced the volume of essays called *The Immense Journey,* he did something of genuine worth in the development of human thought. The more we look at the book the less surprised we are that in *The Times Literary Supplement* (London), it was said, unconditionally, "The appearance of such a book as this is an event." The sensitive reader knows that this judgment is correct if all that he reads is the haunting essay "The Bird and the Machine."

Here is a man who is obviously as competent in the biological sciences as Coulson of Oxford is in mathematical physics and, though the fields are widely different, both have in common a most engaging humility about their respective disciplines. Coulson knows that technology is not enough and Eiseley knows that biology is not enough. He deals, in gentle satire, with all those who affirm dogmatically and pridefully, that we are about to produce life out of nonliving matter.

I have come to suspect that this long descent down the ladder of life, beautiful and instructive though it may be, will not lead us to the final secret. In fact I have ceased to believe in the final brew or the ultimate chemical. There is, I know, a kind of heresy, a shocking negation of our confidence in blue-steel microtomes and men in white in making such a statement. I would not be understood to speak ill of scientific effort, for in simple truth I would not be alive today except for the microscopes and the blue steel. It is only that somewhere among these seeds and beetle shells and abandoned grasshopper legs I find something that is not accounted for very clearly in the dissections to the ultimate virus or crystal or protein particle. Even if the secret is contained in these things, in other words, I do not think it will yield to the kind of analysis our science is capable of making.[13]

This is the kind of writing which can delight the layman because, obviously, it is not the result of superficial acquaintance with the subject, yet it is both a contribution to literature and an evidence of good sense. Only the really competent scientist can point out the limitations of science without inviting the charge of sour grapes. Even if, Eiseley suggests, we do someday produce a living cell out of that which is nonliving, this will not be a world-shaking development. It will only indicate that what we lightly call matter has already contained "amazing, if not dreadful powers." Perhaps it would be only a verification of the guess that matter is "but one mask of the many worn by the Great Face behind."[14] And so the thoughtful scientist, who is clearly more than a scientist, is not worried.

If the day comes when the slime of the laboratory for the first time crawls under man's direction, we shall have great need of humbleness. It will be difficult for us to believe, in our pride of achievement, that the secret of life has slipped through our fingers and eludes us still. We will list all the chemicals and the reactions. The men who have become gods will pose austerely before the popping flashbulbs of news photographers, and there will be few to consider—so deep is the mind-set of an age, whether the desire to link life to matter may not have blinded us to the more remarkable characteristics of both.[15]

When I first read *The Immense Journey* I was deeply puzzled. Whence came the restraint, the genuine humility, the continuing sense of mystery? I knew that these do not arise as necessary ingredients of biology or of anthropology or of any other science, however valuable these disciplines may be. And then, long afterward, I happened to look at the two epigraphs with which the book begins. These epigraphs are quotations, but they were not

[13] *The Immense Journey* (New York: Vintage Books, 1957), p. 202.
[14] *Ibid.*, p. 210.
[15] *Ibid.*, p. 208.

written by anthropologists. One was written by Henry David Thoreau and the other by William Temple. It was primarily the second of these which gave a clue to the solution of my problem. The words were these: "Unless all existence is a medium of revelation, no particular revelation is possible." A man who appreciates the profound paragraph in *Nature, Man and God* from which this sentence is taken is bound to be one who understands more than the details of his own science, for he has a base as well as a field.

CHAPTER 5

The Incendiary Purpose

I came to cast fire upon the earth.
—Luke 12:49

When a Christian expresses sadness about the Church, it is always the sadness of a lover. He knows that there have been great periods and, consequently, he is not willing to settle for anything less than those in his own time. But, though he is saddened by the contrast between what now is and what has been, he is saddened even more by the contrast between all periods and what Christ evidently intended. Whatever else our Lord had in mind, it is clear that He envisioned something very big. He did not propose a slight change in an existing religion! The radical nature of the proposed Church is indicated by the fact that, in one chapter of the New Testament, Christ is reported three times as saying, "Something greater is here" (Matt. 12:6, 41, 42). A small venture would not have aroused such fierce opposition, but neither would it have been worth the trouble. The Christian Movement was initiated as the most radical of all revolutions!

We soon note, as we study the record with this idea in mind, that all of the major Christian figures of speech are indicative of intrinsic bigness. It is the *earth* for which the Church is to be the saving salt. Small as the mustard seed is, at the beginning, its destiny is to become "the greatest" (Matt. 13:32). There is a glorious immodesty in saying "Nothing will be impossible to you" (Matt. 17:21). As we ponder the powerful figure of the leaven, we realize that Christ's aim was not to produce a little sect, which would have been comparatively easy, but to change the entire human enterprise.

The only way to explain the Kingdom is to answer the question, "What is it like?" and Christ answers by saying, "It is like leaven which a woman took and hid in three measures of meal, till it was all leavened" (Luke 13:21). We do not study this passage very long until we see that the crucial word is "all." The Gospel is revolutionary precisely because, when understood, it is always a total Gospel. Harold Loukes, a contemporary English writer, has expressed the magnitude of the central Christian purpose by saying that "the Church is not a tribe for the improvement in holiness of people who think it would be pleasant to be holy, a means to the integration of character for those who cannot bear their conflicts. It is a statement for the divine intention for humanity."[1]

Though the word is shocking to modern man, there is a valid sense in which the Christian Movement must be envisaged as a *violent* one. It is violent because of the enormous break in the conception of what true religion involves. It would not be violent to have slightly better priests, or purified temple practices, or improved synagogue services. Even what John did at the Jordan was really part of the old order, antecedent to the revolution, but not a part of it. "The law and the prophets were until John; since then the good news of the kingdom of God is preached, and every one enters it violently" (Luke 16:16). We shall never have a real renewal of the Church without a serious grappling with this shocking expression. The deepest danger facing the Church is that it may remain pre-Christian. We need all of the help we can get from one another in order to try to understand what it means to enter the Kingdom "violently."

Though the reported words of Christ include many strong figures of speech, each being used in a patient effort to help the uncomprehending to make a start in understanding, the strong-

[1] *The Castle and the Field* (London: George Allen and Unwin, 1959), pp. 55, 57.

est of all figures is the metaphor of the fire, which is printed as the epigraph of this chapter. The figure is so strong that it is almost frightening. Perhaps this is one reason why it is so seldom employed as a text for preaching. It may come to the reader as a surprise to realize that the words of Christ about His incendiary purpose are not even mentioned in Billy Graham's valuable and important book, *World Aflame*. It is equally surprising that Dietrich Bonhoeffer, though he, in writing *The Cost of Discipleship,* mentioned hundreds of Biblical passages, never referred to the text in question. Even more surprising is the fact that the text is not referred to in Samuel Shoemaker's book, *With the Holy Spirit and with Fire*. The text is hard to handle, partly because it represents the complete antithesis to the conventional picture of gentle Jesus, meek and mild. It is the ultimate alternative to mildness.

We are rightly grateful to Luke for preserving the striking sentence in which Christ tells what His basic purpose is. That the sentence expresses basic purpose is indicated by the words "I came." Though the passage is not duplicated in the other canonical Gospels it is found in the recently discovered and partly published *Gospel According to St. Thomas,* and is hinted at by a puzzling expression found in Mark, "For every one will be salted with fire" (9:49).

The references to fire in the Bible involve an instructive development, not unlike that of the figure of the yoke. The yoke is uniformly evil in the Old Testament, a characteristic usage being that of Isaiah 58:6, but in the mouth of Christ, the metaphor is given a genuine novelty so that it provides the clearest meaning of commitment (Matt. 11:29). In a similar way the metaphor of fire is changed. In the Old Testament the characteristic meaning of fire is of something terrible, even though, in the burning bush, it is also glorious. In the New Testament the figure of fire reaches an affirmative climax in the account of Pentecost, the great new experience being so far removed from mildness that it required the use of the fire metaphor to make it clear. "And there appeared to them tongues as of fire, distributed and resting on each one of them" (Acts 2:3).[2]

The bridge between the Old Testament and the New, concerning fire, as also concerning much else, is John the Baptist. One of the most striking aspects of John's recorded ministry is the fact that, however effective he was, he minimized his own contribution in contrast to that which he saw coming. The most vivid expression of the contrast is his statement that, while he baptized with water, his successor would baptize with *fire* (Luke 3:16). It does not take much profundity to see the absolute contrast between the two figures. The difference is not small; it is total!

We cannot, of course, know all that John meant by his emphasis upon fire, but there are helpful hints in his recorded message. It may be that he meant primarily the fire of the Day of Judgment which would purge and consume sinners.[3] If so, Christ seems to have altered the meaning because, when Pentecost finally came, the fire was welcomed and the Church was seen as a body of men and women who were on fire in that their hearts had been kindled at Christ's central fire. The ground was thus prepared for Augustine's famous portrayal of the entire Christian enterprise as that in which one loving heart sets another on fire.

Christ's own statement about His central purpose is remarkable for its double emphasis upon both mood and scope. His single expression is so vividly clear that it makes us understand that the work of Christ's Church, whatever else it may be, must be both flaming in spirit and total in application. It is the "earth," not just the religious element, that requires ignition. It is obvious that this purpose is somehow connected with the experience of baptism. One indication of this is that the author of the Third Gospel follows the fire passage with the words, "I have

[2] The bold new mural, "Miracle at Pentecost," now being painted at Dallas, the finished form of which will be 20 feet high and 124 feet long, will emphasize the tongues of fire. The artist is Torger G. Thomson.

[3] See Samuel Shoemaker, *With the Holy Spirit and with Fire* (New York: Harper & Row, 1960), p. 28.

a baptism to be baptized with" (Luke 12:50).

What did Christ mean by baptism? Evidently He was project-
ing this experience into the future and therefore was not referring back to His own ceremonial baptism by water in the Jordan.
The people who say that all Christians must be immersed, because they are called to be like Christ, and He was immersed, are
making a fundamental mistake, the essence of their mistake
being the failure to take seriously Christ's metaphorical use of
the baptismal experience.

Among those who have struggled most passionately with the
meaning of Baptism by Fire is Walter Russell Bowie. He lays
emphasis upon Christ's coming agony when he says:

> One cannot read these words of Jesus without awe. It is as
> though one were permitted for a moment to look into the infinite
> arena where Jesus wrestled with the terrible issues which His soul
> confronted. "I have a baptism to be baptized with." Now a bap-
> tism not of water, but of blood. He was going up to Jerusalem to
> face hostility and fury, to precipitate a conflict that would cause
> fire on the earth. That fire would be the devastating challenge of
> God's spirit to the pride and sin of men, and he who carried that
> fire would have to be baptized in a devotion unto death.[4]

Though this is nobly said, it does not go far enough. There
was to be the fire of lonely suffering, but there was to be much
more beyond this. The central fire, as it scattered, was destined to
enkindle other and lesser fires and thus to cause an unending
chain reaction. Conventionally the reference to baptism in Luke
12:50 has been seen as referring merely to Christ's death, with the
curious omission of the emphasis on evangelism. But we must
make the further connection if we are to take Luke's juxtaposi-
tion of the two sentences (12:49 and 12:50) seriously. When
Christ died He *did scatter fire,* because many new fires were
started as a consequence. Perhaps the incendiary conception of
the atonement can be a help to many mystified but open-minded

[4] *The Compassionate Christ* (Nashville: Abingdon Press, 1965) p. 181.

seekers. It may make sense to them because it is so obviously an interpretation of experience.

The actual incendiary result of Christ's death and resurrection as recorded in the New Testament is really very impressive. Whatever else we can say about the fellowship, it was certainly intense. Not only did it produce Pentecost, with its "tongues as of fire"; it also led Christians to a sharing which was so profound that they accepted, for a time, unlimited economic liability for one another. All this they did "with glad and generous hearts" (Acts 2:46). The fellowships described in the Epistles were far from perfect, many sins being freely recognized, but they were, in any case, centers of power. The one thing which these people really knew was "the power of his resurrection" (Phil. 3:10). Sinful and inadequate as they clearly were, those who experienced corporately the baptism by fire worked together. Their evangelism was nearly always implemented as a team ministry and their travels, in which they faced severe hardships, were shared experiences. We fail, sometimes, to see how exciting the early Christian fellowship was, because we read back into the account our own contemporary and conventional church experience.

To understand Christ's baptism we must understand His relation to John. Somehow, John, with his prediction of baptism by fire, is involved. We see this by the subsequent reference to John in Christ's last earthly appearance (Acts 1:5). Christ's relation to John was undoubtedly complex. The quality of His admiration for John was indicated by the expression, "He was a burning and shining lamp" (John 5:35), yet he was not really a part of the new emerging order. The double character of Christ's judgment of John is indicated by the sentence, "I tell you, among those born of women none is greater than John; yet he who is least in the kingdom of God is greater than he" (Luke 7:28). William Temple helps us to appreciate the contrast by emphasizing the difference which is involved in the metaphors of water and fire. To be baptized by water is the merely symbolic experience of being cleansed or forgiven; to be baptized by fire is to be *ignited*. "The one," writes Temple, "is a mere cleansing from past contamination with the possibility of a new beginning; the latter is a positive energy of righteousness, a consuming flame of purity."[5]

It is the judgment of many scholars that the similar accounts of John's preaching, preserved by Matthew and Luke, are from a lost document which we call Q and that the original version in this was "baptize with fire." If so, baptism by fire came, partly as a result of the experience at Pentecost, to be interpreted by the early Church as the baptism of the Holy Spirit.[6] If John invented the phrase "baptism by fire," it is probable that he did not see all that was involved in this exciting expression. Specifically, he seems to have stressed the fierceness of destruction rather than the subsequent idea of an evangelistic chain reaction.

If John thought of the divine fire as primarily that which consumes, it is not surprising, because this interpretation was in line with his heritage. Naturally he was familiar with Isaiah 66:15, "For behold, the Lord will come in fire, and his chariots like the stormwind, to render his anger in fury, and his rebuke with flames of fire." In similar vein he would know Jeremiah 6:29, "The bellows blow fiercely, the lead is consumed by the fire." This interpretation of the divine action is not lacking even in the New Testament as when we read, in Hebrews 12:29, "Our God is a consuming fire." A similar usage is that of II Peter 3:7, 10. Though there is a certain validity to this emphasis, we cannot appreciate Christ's vision of the character of His Church unless we see His intention as fire-bringer in far larger terms. All who love the Church and who pray for its fulfillment can be grateful to Dr. Bowie for his statement of what it might mean to men if the fire of Christ were really to start blazing on the earth. "It would," he says, "be a fire of affliction in which their courage would be tested, as gold in the furnace is tried; a fire on the altar

---

[5] *Readings in St. John's Gospel, op. cit.*, p. 22.
[6] See Robert H. Mounce, *The Essential Nature of New Testament Preaching* (Grand Rapids: William B. Eerdman's Publishing Company, 1960), p. 23.

of sacrifice where fear and selfishness could be burned away. It would also be like the light of a lamp to illumine their minds and consciences; and a flame within their hearts to burn there as unquenchable devotion."[7]

The miracle of the early Church was a partial fulfillment of Christ's expressed purpose about setting the earth on fire. Of course this did not involve all of mankind, but there is no doubt that the fire burned brightly enough, in the lives of those who were involved in the Movement, to make a miraculous difference in the culture of the ancient world. What we know is that it was the incendiary character of the early Christian fellowship which was amazing to the contemporary Romans and that it was amazing precisely because there was nothing in their experience that was remotely similar to it. Religion they had in vast quantities, but it was nothing like this. Consequently the Romans, even the best of them, had no inkling of what was coming in the message of the early Church. Ceremonies they had galore, even Julius Caesar being a chief priest, but "Religion in the first century, B.C., had no stirring message of hope for the masses of Rome."[8]

The metaphor of the fire would be meaningless without the fellowship, because it has no significance for merely individual religion, as it has none for merely ceremonial religion. Though it is, of course, impossible to have a committed Church with uncommitted members, the major power never appears except in a shared experience. Much of the uniqueness of Christianity, in its original emergence, consisted of the fact that simple people could be amazingly powerful when they were members one of another. As everyone knows, it is almost impossible to create a fire with one log, even if it is a sound one, while several poor logs may make an excellent fire if they stay together as they burn. The miracle of the early Church was that of poor sticks making a

---

[7] *Men of Fire* (New York: Harper & Row, 1961), p. ix.

[8] F. R. Cowell, *Cicero and the Roman Republic* (New York: Chanticleer Press, 1948), p. 273. Note that the Romans appreciated the figure of the fire in other connections. Pitt translated a Latin epigram as follows: "Eloquence is like the flame. It requires fuel to feed it, motion to excite it, and it brightens as it burns."

grand conflagration. A good fire glorifies even its poorest fuel.

A fuller consideration of Christ's metaphor helps us to understand the importance of each humble and unworthy member of the total flaming fellowship. Many, when they tell frankly how their lives have been changed, refer to the faith and witness of some wholly obscure person who has been the instrument of ignition. This is why the Church is so important and why there can never be a Churchless Christianity. There is no Gospel in general. What we have in fact is always the Gospel according to somebody. The evangelists of the New Testament did not stand alone in their vocation, but were merely early representatives of a practice which has been maintained to this day, for an uninterpreted Christ is something wholly unknown to anybody. One of the most quotable of William Temple's many quotable sentences is that in which he stressed the mutual dependence of Christian people. "It is by the faith of others," he said, "that our faith is kindled."[9]

Though Christ's statement of His incendiary purpose has been strangely neglected, there have been reflections of it at various high moments in the history of the Church. There is a hint of the central purpose in Romans 12:11, which, in the Revised Standard Version, reads, "Be aglow with the Spirit." Dr. Phillips connects it more closely with Christ's announced purpose with, "Let us keep the fires of the spirit burning." When Blaise Pascal needed language to express the vivid character of his life-changing experience in November, 1654, he wrote in large letters, on his secret document, the word FIRE. In the succeeding century John Wesley picked up the same theme with the well-known words, "My heart was strangely warmed." A prayer which comes out of the anonymous depths of the Church and which has been effectively employed by Nels Ferré is:

> Come as the fire and burn,
> Come as the wind and cleanse,
> Come as a light and reveal.

[9] *Readings in St. John's Gospel, op. cit.,* p. xvi.

> Convict, convert, consecrate,
> Until we are wholly thine.

Only a faith of which such a prayer is a valid expression can make the required difference in any civilization. Mild religion cannot sustain itself because it cannot start even a tiny flame.

In our own day we have learned, with some surprise, of the power of the Church which emerged in connection with the consecration of the new Cathedral at Coventry. This has been told in the book by Stephen Verney, with the singularly appropriate title, *Fire in Coventry,* to which we have already alluded. The book is a simple and straightforward account of how one sector of Christ's Church began to glow twenty years after the disastrous blitz which destroyed the old Cathedral. The later fire was as renewing as the earlier fire had been destructive.

There are several features of the new Coventry fire which are truly surprising. One is that the main experience came within the Anglican communion, which is usually considered as having no spark at all. Another surprise is that the people provided the leadership themselves rather than bring in outside professional evangelists. The central mission, that of April 4 to 14, 1962, was led by the Bishop himself and was preceded by a tour of the diocese in which he met all of the leaders, both lay and clergy, kindling enthusiasm as he went. The Bishop knew that a fire does not exist without the collection and preparation of fuel. It is not probable that he was familiar with the words of the seventeenth-century Quaker and ship's captain, Robert Fowler, who wrote, laconically, in the log of the *Woodhouse,* "They gathered sticks, and kindled a fire, and left it burning." Fowler was referring to the evangelistic work of the passengers of his vessel who, when they interrupted their voyage for a while on the south coast of England, employed their time by careful efforts to spread the fire which was raging in their own lives. Whether the Bishop of Coventry knew of this expression or not, he certainly borrowed a Quaker practice, as the following account shows:

When the Bishop had finished speaking, we had on each occasion a remarkable period of prayer. "I am going to ask you," he said, "to do what you have probably never done before in your life. To pray out loud, in your own words. We shall wait upon God in silence, and each of us is free to offer up prayer as we wish."[10]

As we read Canon Verney's book we have in our hands something far more valuable than a brilliant speculation about the means by which the Church might be renewed; we have an account of how renewal has actually taken place in one specific area. We learn how a great many people learned to pray, singly and together; we learn how the people became involved in an effort and were not merely observers of a stunning spectacle, planned by professionals. The near-total involvement of the laity was crucial. "The laity had come to see, with a shock," says Verney, "that they were the representatives of Christ who were actually present in the factories, shops, offices, schools and homes of the country. If Christ's compassion was to get into these situations, then they, the laity, must be the channels through which it would come. If Christ's truth was to be spoken, then they must speak it."[11] The first clear answer to the many prayers was the involvement of the people. "The more deeply people were involved, the more clearly was God calling them to go deeper still, and to offer him the obedience of their whole lives."[12]

The fire of Christ did not really burn in Coventry until the Gospel was total, not only in that it involved all of the people, but also in that it referred to every aspect of their lives. The fire could not burn brightly if religion was seen as something separate from ordinary lives. The fire would not be genuine if it were concentrated merely in the great new building.

During the next three weeks we experienced an extraordinary outburst of worship and happiness as the whole diocese celebrated a festival from end to end. Great services were held in the

[10] *Op. cit.*, p. 33.
[11] *Ibid.*, p. 25.
[12] *Ibid.*, p. 35.

new Cathedral, offering up to God every part of our daily lives. There were services for Industry and Agriculture, for Schools, for Local Government, the Armed Forces, Youth, Old Age Pensioners and the Medical Services, to mention only a few.[13]

The value, for us, of the story of the new Coventry fire is that it restores hope. All who visited Coventry immediately after the war have some idea how great the change has been. If the miracle could occur at Coventry, why not anywhere? But it will never come without a heightened vision of what the mission of the Church is. It is literally true that where there is no exalted vision the Church languishes. Nothing happened at Coventry until a few began to see that there was "a great people to be gathered," and until they sensed the glory of a sanctified people who were one in Christ. Once they had this disturbing vision, they gathered to pray and they shared their vision with other people until they had a sufficient number of human allies in their redemptive effort. Our major heresy in many areas of the life of the Church today, is that we do not really believe that a result of such magnitude is possible.

As we meditate upon the Coventry experience, we begin to see what the essence of evangelism is, and we realize that we cannot state it adequately without reference to Christ's disturbing metaphor. *Evangelism occurs when people are so enkindled by contact with the central fire of Christ that they, in turn, set others on fire.* The only adequate evidence that anything is on fire is the pragmatic evidence that other fires are started by it. A fire that does not spread must eventually go out! This is the point of Emil Brunner's dictum that "the Church exists by mission as fire exists by burning." A person who claims to have a religious experience, yet makes no effort to share or to extend it, has not really entered into Christ's Company at all. In short, an unevangelistic or unmissionary Christianity is a contradiction in terms. If we did not know this by other means we should know it by pondering Christ's statement of His incendiary purpose.

[13] *Ibid.,* p. 49.

In a day when there are many things to discourage us, there is real encouragement in the renewed acceptance of Christian evangelism which was once supposed to be obsolete. It is not insignificant that Billy Graham has spoken directly to more human beings than has any other living person. Not all of these have listened, but some have done so and others, with different gifts, are recognizing the intrinsic necessity of Christian evangelism. The obsolete man is the alleged Christian who proudly says, "I keep my faith to myself." The late Samuel Shoemaker spoke for an entire generation when he said, as a reflection of his own experience, "There is no Church where evangelism is not living and current."[14]

We are developing today a new breed of Christian spokesmen who, though they are undoubted intellectuals, are not in the least ashamed to express warmly the love of Christ and to engage in evangelistic effort. A good example of this new breed is Bishop Gerald Kennedy of Los Angeles, but he by no means stands alone.[15] In nearly every instance this new combination of intellectual power and evangelical warmth has come by a deeper study of the New Testament. It is hard to peruse this amazing book in depth and not begin to realize that the early Church, in its period of greatest vitality, was very different from most parts of the conventional Church in our own day. Perhaps the most striking feature, from our contemporary point of view, is that *all* of the early Christians were missionaries. They did not leave the evangelistic task either to professional evangelists or to pastors to whom they paid salaries, for these did not exist. As we read the truly exciting story of the early Church, persevering as it did in the face of incredible odds, we sense the difference between the task of merely *supporting* missionaries and of *being* missionaries. The early Church did not *have* a missionary arm; it *was* a missionary movement. The Church was, more than anything else, a missionary band. Judged by this high standard the contemporary Church has very little reason for complacency or pride.

[14] *Op. cit.,* p. 67.
[15] See Bishop Kennedy's news note in the *Christian Advocate* (July 28, 1966), p. 21.

We have denied our vocation by the acceptance of a division of labor. There are situations, as Plato points out in the *Republic,* in which a division of labor is a necessity for any genuine civilization, but there are other situations in which such separation of effort can mean defeat. It always means defeat if we allow religion to be a professional job of a few experts, with the rank and file relieved of all responsibility. Though it is unreasonable to expect each man to be a qualified engineer, it is not unreasonable to expect each church member to learn to pray and also to learn to tell others of how the love of Christ has reached his life. Neither prayer nor witness is easy or is quickly learned, but both are, by their very nature, part of the vocation of every lay Christian.

We make an important forward step when we learn to distinguish, as Churchmen, between profession and vocation. The idea of a profession is necessary for the existence of any civilization, because there are tasks which require disciplined competence. We have seen, for a long time, that professional group concern is a chief means of maintaining standards in law, in medicine, in engineering, in literature, and in much more. A professional is one who takes pride in performing, with excellence, a particular work, being willing to pay the price of arduous study over extended periods, in order to learn the lessons taught by predecessors in the same skill. We are grateful for the professional societies which police their own members, expose charlatans, and reward competence by recognition.

Instead of rejecting professionalism, Christians should encourage it in all fields in which it is appropriate or relevant. Some of these fields are in the work of the Church. Thus we need men who take a professional stance in developing their powers of speaking, of writing, and of counseling. There is nothing wrong in learning professionally how to be a good pastor, in the sense of being the coach of the team as developed in Chapter 2 of this book. On the whole the professional does better at such a task than does the amateur, no matter how gifted the latter may be.

In the Church, even more than in the world, it is important that each task be done well rather than clumsily, because there is so much at stake. The Christian writer must discipline himself to write clearly, and the Christian speaker must discipline himself to speak convincingly. The fact that we are dealing with holy things does not mean that piety can take the place of costly competence. A Christian magazine should be as well edited as is a secular one. In short, we need all of the professional excellence which we can get. But vocation is a different matter. While only a few Christians are called to professional journalism, every Christian is called to the vocation of being Christ's representative in his time and place. All must pray, even though some may do it haltingly or ungrammatically. "Consider your call, brethren; not many of you were wise according to worldly standards, not many were powerful" (I Cor. 1:26). The universality of Christian vocation means that, over and over, God chooses what is weak to shame the strong and that He can use those who have no professional religious skills. This is how it was in the glorious early days of the Christian Movement, and it must always be so again if renewal is to be genuine.

Renewal will not come merely by the acts of professional renewers or by hierarchial operations; it will come only when Christians understand and implement the idea that vocation is universal. Renewal does not come unless the members accept unreservedly and unapologetically the fact that each one is called to be a member of Christ's team. There are meant to be exactly as many missionaries and evangelists as there are members. To be a missionary need not mean to go away from home, while to be an evangelist need not mean necessarily the development of persuasive public speech. Instead each means engagement in Operation Ignition. The only way to be loyal to the fire of Christ is to spread it.

Much of our present danger is that we do not see our task in its proper magnitude. Even when we accept the basic figure of the fire, we tend to interpret our vocation as that of husbanding the little flame in the effort to keep it flickering a little longer. What we ought to know is that a flame cannot, in its very nature, be contained. Without growth extinguishment is inevitable, because, with fire, there is no third way. As salt cannot fulfill its vocation except as it loses itself in the meat, so fire cannot continue to burn unless it penetrates the surrounding combustible material. Perhaps it was this basic similarity of the two striking figures, relative to the Church, which caused Christ to combine them and to say, "For every one will be salted with fire" (Mark 9:49). Why Mark preserved this and why it was not picked up by Matthew and Luke we do not know. Perhaps the paradox was too mystifying.

The Church cannot fulfill its sacred vocation unless it is a penetrating force, as salt is, and the penetration cannot even begin unless the fellowship which is the Church has something of the character of an explosion. Little can be done with a smoldering fire; somehow there must be a blaze. But how is this to be achieved? We do not know all of the answers to this practical question, but we know something. Since the starter of the fire is Christ Himself, our initial means of achieving a real blaze is that of confronting Him as steadily and as directly as is humanly possible. When the closeness to Christ is lost, the fire either goes out or it merely smolders, like the fires in the great swamps which are hidden from the sun. A Christianity which ceases to be Christ-centered may have some other valuable features, but it is usually lacking in power.

To confront Christ is really to allow Him to confront us, both as a group and singly, for we are changed by direct acquaintance. Fortunately, this is made possible, in part, by the incredibly valuable accounts preserved in the Gospels. These we can study scientifically, as well as devotionally, and the reader is almost sure to be deeply moved by both approaches. If any sincere seeker will try the experiment of reading the Gospels for a year, slowly and consecutively, but, above all, prayerfully and also with an open mind, it is practically certain that something of importance will occur in his life. If he stays close enough, for a sufficiently long period, to the central fire, he is likely to be ignited himself. But, since Christ is alive, we need not be limited to the written word. He is really as close to any humble searcher now as He was to Andrew and Simon by the Sea of Galilee. The history of the Church, in all of its most vital periods, has been a continual verification of the prediction that, if anyone hears His voice and opens the door, He will come in (Rev. 3:20).

It is right that the Church should be concerned with human problems, such as those of poverty and housing and education, but unless there is a recurring effort to keep close to the Source of inspiration for such work in the world, something of crucial importance will be lacking. The notion that we must choose between being service-centered and Christ-centered is a wholly confused notion. In fact, we shall not long continue to be service-centered if we cease to be Christ-centered.

One result of confrontation with Christ, by every means available, is that there comes a striking increase in courage in the face of the intellectual attacks which we must face. When, for example, the Christian is challenged, about the employment of prayer, by those who accept uncritically the current naturalism, he has an answer. When he is told that prayer, especially at a distance, cannot possibly be effective, because of the reign of natural law, according to which physical events are already determined even before we pray, the Churchman who has sought to confront Christ daily can answer that there is evidence that Christ prayed.[16] Indeed, this is one of the most revealing features of the entire Gospel. If Christ prayed, and if He prayed for material things as well as for spiritual ones, the Christian is not easily intimidated by his confident critics. The Christian does not need to claim to know all of the answers but, in staying close to the example of Christ, he is convinced that the answers are possible.

We cannot, in our finitude, produce the desired ignition, but we can do much to hinder it, just as we can keep the door closed, even when there is a continual knocking. One of our chief ways of hindering the fire is by nourishing a fear of emotion. In many sectors of the Church there is still, even at this day, real timidity

[16] I have sought to deal carefully with this theme in *The Lord's Prayers* (New York: Harper & Row, 1965).

about any expression of the love of Christ. It is somehow felt that such an expression denies a person entrance into the intellectual club. This is why, in some circles, the singing of evangelical hymns is virtually taboo. There are congregations in which the people have not, for ten years, sung "Jesus, Lover of My Soul." What these people are doing, without being conscious of it, amounts to an effort to insulate their lives and thus to *prevent* the fire from being kindled in their cold hearts.

Fortunately we are seeing the beginning of a change. There is emerging among us a new style of Christian living, in which the adolescent fear of emotion is being overcome. The men who are beginning to give the most potent contemporary Christian leadership are *rational evangelicals,* who recognize no difficulty whatever in being both hardheaded on intellectual problems and warmhearted in their love of Christ. Far from being fearful of passion, these men are well aware that nothing of importance is ever created without it. Certainly we could have no great poetry without passion. Intense caring, far from hindering intellectual integrity, supports and encourages it. Accordingly, while we need many kinds of courage, our supreme need is of the courage to care.

One interesting evidence of the new mood, which indicates some outgrowing of the fear of religious emotion, is found in the new hymnals, particularly *The Methodist Hymnal,* just published. This, which is probably more widely distributed than is any other, now restores to the Number One position Charles Wesley's "O For a Thousand Tongues to Sing." The preceding edition had demoted Wesley's moving appeal from its prominent position, and this was a revelation of a mood which we can say, gratefully, is beginning to pass. There are, of course, so-called evangelical hymns which ought to be rejected because they are musically poor or merely sentimental in tone, but there is a singular lack of maturity in the judgment which, because of this, rejects all hymns which express a Christ-centered passion. Whether or not the authors had Christ's words in mind we do not know, but several of the best hymns reflect the figure of

Christ as the starter of a conflagration. Note the phrase "a living fire" in "My Faith Looks Up to Thee," and the magnificent ending of "Spirit of God, Descend upon My Heart" in the words, "My heart an altar, and Thy love the flame."

Though we are now beginning to see the general acceptance of a "rational evangelicalism," this has long been known in individuals who have not represented the prevailing mood. William Temple referred, in such terms, to his own father, Frederick Temple, who was also Archbishop of Canterbury and whose grave lies next to that of his famous son in the Cathedral courtyard. The son said his father was described by one who knew him as "granite on fire."[17] Though far from a sentimentalist, Frederick Temple could not speak of the love of God without tears. John Huess, who died while rector of Trinity Church, New York, expressed the encouraging new mood of the Church when he said that what we need is "quiet fanatics." The combination is, indeed, a paradox, but it is in paradox that the deepest truth normally is found. In fact, the Gospel is always combining contrasting features into creative wholes. Christ is loving, but He brings a sword; the disciple must exhibit both quietness and power. Thus the truth is never really simple. Perhaps that is why we can touch only the hem of His garment, but to touch even the hem is something of vast importance.

It is always encouraging to be able to point to individuals who exhibit the combination of toughness and tenderness which we so sorely need in the life of the Church. Here, for instance, is an astronomer who has disciplined his eyes and his mind to interpret the findings of a telescope, as no layman can, yet he is one whose loyalty to Christ is expressed with the unconsciousness of a little child. The exciting fact is that this combination is not only logically possible, but is actually observed in experience. Few, in the last century, have exhibited this desirable combination more vividly than did Professor Rendel Harris. He was one of the brightest lights in the galaxy of minds which adorned Johns Hopkins University at the end of the nineteenth century, yet, at

[17] *Readings in St. John's Gospel, op. cit.,* p. xv.

the same time, he sang and prayed with the fervor of an early follower of Christ. He could move, with no sense of incongruity, from the critical analysis of some ancient manuscript to the prayer meeting in his home, in which he always dropped to his knees. He loved the truth and he loved Christ, and he saw not the slightest incompatibility between the two kinds of passion.[18]

As we seek to recover the richness of the Gospel metaphor of the fire, we can be assisted by modern technological developments. Since fire is now spread by a charge on an electric wire, we need to consider the conditions of its transfer. The important fact to observe, in this connection, is that, if the charge on the wire is too weak, *nothing* comes through. Applying the modern metaphor, we may say that a little commitment turns out to be the same as none. There has to be more charge on the wire if we are to have any valuable result at all. If the fire does not get hotter it might as well be extinguished.

The glorious fact is that there *can* be more charge on the wire and that it will come, providing we permit it. Our hope is kept bright by the way in which the flames leap up, at various points in human history, when men, themselves, are sufficiently obedient to meet the conditions. One of the most striking examples of the way in which the fire of Christ can burn brightly is that of a loving fellowship made up of modest persons of the seventeenth century who were part of what was fundamentally an experiment in Christian renewal. The explosive power of this fellowship, which led eventually to successive attacks on a variety of social evils, was expressed in a torrent of written words, many of which have been preserved. Each gathering was likely to be a time of wonder and of consequent power. Men and women, when arrested because of illegal religious assemblies, went to prison gladly and experienced some truly electrifying meetings behind prison walls. Perhaps the most brilliant single statement of the incendiary theme was that of Francis Howgill (1618-1669), whose description of the new corporate experience was preserved in the

---

[18] An example of the creative union of the two moods in the work of this scholar is *The Sufferings and the Glory* (London: Headley Brothers).

preliminary leaves of the collected works of Edward Burrough (1633-1663). Even the title of the book indicated the mood; it was called *The Memorable Works of a Son of Thunder*. Howgill's words are so valuable that they should be known by every serious follower of Christ.

The Kingdom of Heaven did gather us and catch us all, as in a net, and his heavenly power at one time drew many hundreds to land. We came to know a place to stand in and what to wait in; and the Lord appeared daily to us, to our astonishment, amazement and great admiration, insomuch that we often said one unto another with great joy of heart: "What, is the Kingdom of God come to be with men? And will he take up his tabernacle among the sons of men, as he did of old? Shall we, that were reckoned as the outcasts of Israel, have this honour of glory communicated amongst us, which were but men of small parts and of little abilities, in respect of many others, as amongst men?" And from that day forward, our hearts were knit unto the Lord and one unto another in true and fervent love, in the covenant of Life with God; and that was a strong obligation or bond upon all our spirits, which united us one unto another. We met together in the unity of the Spirit, and of the bond of peace, treading down under our feet all reasoning about religion. And holy resolutions were kindled in our hearts as a fire which the Life kindled in us to serve the Lord while we had a being, and mightily did the Word of God grow amongst us, and the desires of many were after the Name of the Lord. O happy day! O blessed day! the memorial of which can never pass out of my mind. And thus the Lord, in short, did form us to be a people for his praise in our generation.[19]

This kind of experience of a genuine fellowship in the Living Christ ought to be the standard of expectation, rather than the

[19] These words took hold of me in an incendiary way when I read them, sixteen years ago, in the old meetinghouse at Yealand Conyers, in the community associated with the life of Edward Burrough. The experience gave me a deep dissatisfaction with the contemporary Church.

exception. Because this is true, we can see clearly that low ex-
pectancy is a sin. We cannot and need not repeat the external
circumstances of people in the period of England's Commonwealth,
but we ought to be ashamed of acquiescence in any lower standard. We have made at least a start on renewal of vision, which is
the prime renewal we need, when we understand that the
Church is meant to be an incendiary fellowship and nothing
less.